The American Association of Patriots Presents

HOW TO TALK TO YOUR CAT ABOUT GUN SAFETY

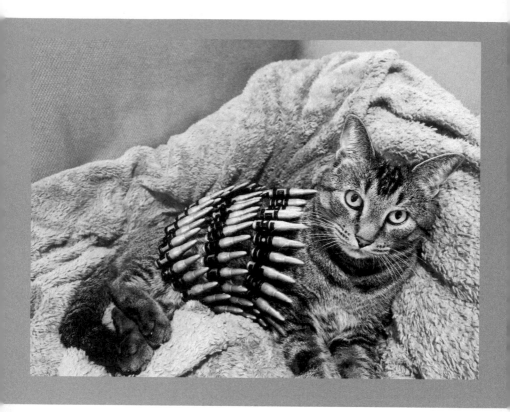

The American Association of Patriots Presents

HOW TO TALK TO YOUR CAT ABOUT GUN SAFETY

And Abstinence, Drugs, Satanism, and Other Dangers That Threaten Their Nine Lives

THREE RIVERS PRESS
NEW YORK

All rights reserved.
Published in the United States by Three Rivers Press,
an imprint of the Crown Publishing Group, a division of
Penguin Random House LLC, New York.
www.crownpublishing.com

Three Rivers Press and the Tugboat design are registered
trademarks of Penguin Random House LLC.

The following chapters, "How to Talk to Your Cat About Gun Safety," "How to Talk
to Your Cat About Evolution," and "How to Talk to Your Cat About Abstinence,"
were first published in print 'zine form.

Library of Congress Cataloging-in-Publication Data
Names: Auburn, Zachary.
    Title: The American Association of Patriots presents
    How to talk to your cat about gun safety / Zachary Auburn.
    Other titles: How to talk to your cat about gun safety
    Description: First edition. | New York : Three Rivers Press, 2016.
    Identifiers: LCCN 2016004002 | ISBN 9780451494924 (paperback)
    Subjects: LCSH: Cats--Humor. | Conservatism--Humor. | Parodies. | BISAC:
    HUMOR / Form / Parodies. | HUMOR / Topic / Animals. | HUMOR / Topic /
    Political.
    Classification: LCC PN6231.C23 A93 2016 | DDC 818/.602--dc23 LC
    record available at http://lccn.loc.gov/2016004002

ISBN 978-0-451-49492-4
eBook ISBN 978-0-451-49493-1

Printed in the United States of America

Book design by Andrea Lau
Cover design by Alane Gianetti
Cover photograph: (cat) albaraa/Flickr; (gun) kcdstm/Flickr

30 29 28 27 26 25 24 23 22 21

First Edition

The American Association of Patriots would like to dedicate this book to

Jason at Floating World

Chloe at Reading Frenzy

Kevin at Powell's Books

Jenn at Skylight Books

Rachel at Atomic Books

Joshua at Antiquated Future

and all the other patriotic booksellers
who make America great

CONTENTS

INTRODUCTION

My fellow *purrtriots*,

You hold in your hands the only book in print today with the courage to tell it like it is. To stand up to the idolaters, the liberals, the international bankers, and the secret kings of Europe who want to destroy America and replace it with their one-world government. To bring about our downfall, these villains have targeted what is surely our greatest national resource: our cats. They know that no other cats in the world are as cute as ours. American cats have the softest bellies, the fluffiest tails, and the loudest purrs. We are the greatest country in the history of the world, and we have the cats to match. Our enemies know they have no chance of defeating us while we stand tall with our cats by our sides, and so for years these scoundrels have worked in the shadows, trying to weaken us and our cats. Stripping from our cats their Second Amendment right to bear arms! Undermining the faith of our kittens by teaching them the lie of evolution! Addicting our feline friends to the scourge of catnip! The cats of America are under siege. Whether they are hiding in their favorite cardboard box, climbing a tree, or napping in a sunbeam, our cats are under attack. And they desperately need our help.

This book is a compilation of the eight brochures that we have deemed most important to maintaining the well-being of our cats, body and soul. Our country—and our cats—stands at a precipice. Will we rise to the challenge and forge our nation into a shining beacon of liberty that would make our Founding Fathers proud?

It will take courage, and it will take hard work, but armed with the knowledge contained within these pages, you and your cats can make America great again!

With constant vigilance,

ZACHARY AUBURN
PRESIDENT OF THE AMERICAN ASSOCIATION OF PATRIOTS

HOW TO TALK TO
YOUR CAT ABOUT
GUN SAFETY

AMERICAN ASSOCIATION OF PATRIOTS

Do I need to talk to my cat about gun safety?

The first question many of you will be asking is, "Do I really need to teach my cat about gun safety?" The answer is an unequivocal "Yes!!!" The Constitution of the United States of America guarantees us the right to own and operate firearms, and that is a right we *must* exercise in order to keep our country healthy, lest our democracy atrophy. It is the duty of all American citizens—as well as their cats—to be able to use and maintain a firearm. Citizens who cannot handle a gun safely are as irresponsible and useless as citizens who do not own a gun at all. Americans and their homes are under attack. It is im*purr*ative that, in order to ensure the future security of our country, every man, woman, child, and cat be able to defend our nation against the enemies of democracy.

Do cats really play with guns?

Yes! Absolutely yes! Even a cursory search of the Internet will turn up dozens of pictures of cats playing with guns, almost all handling them in an incredibly unsafe manner. The pictures scattered throughout this pamphlet are but a small sample—the tip of the iceberg—that illustrates the very real danger posed by cats who are uneducated in the ways of gun safety.

So my cat finds a gun, what's the big deal?

It is frequently said that curiosity killed the cat, but what is often left *un*said is that the actual cause of death was the improper discharge of a firearm by a poorly trained feline. Cats are inquisitive creatures, no doubt about it. They are going to explore every nook and cranny of your home. And if you keep a firearm in your place of residence (which you should), it is only a matter of time before your cat discovers it. *Pawse* for a *meowment* to think about which scenario you would rather have play out:

Your cat, never having seen or handled a gun before, bats it around as if it's just another toy or stuffed mouse, possibly discharging it in the process?

Or,

Your cat, whom you have already talked to about how a firearm is a tool and not a toy, and who has received extensive training on the proper handling of the weapon, discovers your firearm and accords it the respect it is due?

The answer should be as obvious as the whiskers on your cat's face!

Is it safe to own a gun if I have cats in my house?

*Paw*sitively yes! A gun is a tool, plain and simple. While it does have the potential to cause injury, the same is true of cleaning chemicals, knives, and matches. It is only because of the propaganda and scare tactics of the liberal, Zionist-run media that Americans second-guess the wisdom of keeping guns in their homes—scare tactics that undoubtedly serve their greater agenda to overthrow the rightful leadership of the United States, and the subsequent imposition of a European-based one-world government. If anything, once you have explained to your cat the im*purr*tance of responsible gun handling, having a firearm in your home will make your cat considerably safer. Not only will your fluffy little friend be prepared to fend off criminal, foreign, or supernatural threats, but cats from gun-free homes are more likely to be curious about weapons they encounter than cats who are already familiar with them. As we will discuss in the next section, it is impossible to guarantee that your cat will never come into contact with a gun, so make sure your kitty is ready for it when that day finally arrives!

I'm responsible with my gun, why should I bother to teach my cat about gun safety?

You always keep your guns unloaded when not in use. They are stored in a secured gun safe that only you have the key to. You even have trigger locks. Surely with all these precautions you don't need to talk to your cat about responsible firearm usage, right? Wrong. Dead wrong! Even if you keep your firearms se-cure, that doesn't mean your cat won't encounter one elsewhere, especially if they're an outside cat. Do you really know what your cat is up to when they leave the house? What other cats they associate with? Where they go? What they're doing? While 40 percent of American households are smart enough to own at least one firearm, not all of them are as responsible as you. Think about how many homes on your block alone might have unsecured weapons your cat could get their paws on. Even worse, many of these unsecured guns are kept in cardboard boxes, a container most cats will find irresistible. If your pet were to come into contact with a gun without the proper training, it could be a *catastrophe*!

ADVICE FROM OUR EX*PURR*TS

All the guns in the world won't do your cat a lick of good if he doesn't have the am*mew*nition to back them up. Wrapping your cat in a bandolier will help ensure he's ready for trouble wherever he goes, whether it's out in the neighborhood, using his litter box, or even snuggled in his favorite blanket.

What is the best age to start talking to my cat about gun safety?

The easy answer is that no age is too young to start introducing your cat to the benefits and responsibilities of gun ownership, but realistically, you should wait until at least a week after birth, when cats begin to open their eyes. At no point in your cat's life will it be more playful and precocious than when they're a kitten. The obituaries are filled with families who thought that their kitten was too young to play with guns, that they could wait until the cat was just a little bit older to instruct them on proper firearm usage and safety. This assumption is irresponsible, and—too often—fatal! If anything, the youthfulness of your kitten is even more reason to teach them about firearms. Never forget: your kitten's curiosity, clumsiness, mischievousness, and lack of problem-solving abilities can be a deadly combination!

Just like your cat uses a scratching post to keep her claws sharp, taking her to a shooting range several times a week will help keep her skills sharp. Remember, practice makes *purrfect*!

What are the risks of not talking to my cat about gun safety?

Every day that you hesitate in talking to your cat about gun safety you are putting yourself, your loved ones, and your cat at risk. Think about your cat, sitting by a window, watching a bird in a nearby tree. How much does your cat want to catch that bird!? They desire nothing more, and if your cat has not been trained to respect the power of a firearm, they may use your gun to do it!

You might think that there's no danger in this, that cats are natural hunters. But until your cat has practiced in the controlled setting of a reputable and licensed firing range, you cannot assume that they have the skills necessary to operate the gun safely. While cats do possess many innate skills when it comes to hunting, the operation of a firearm is not among them. Over 40 percent of firearm accidents involving cats are caused by improperly trained felines attempting to shoot birds out of trees: accidents that lead to the wounding or death of tens of thousands of humans and cats every single year. This is the most common danger you expose your household to when you fail to talk to your cat about gun safety, but it's certainly not the only one. Don't procatstinate! Talk to your cat today!

Wait, does that mean that I shouldn't allow my cat to use a gun while hunting?

No, of course your cat should have access to all the weaponry our Founding Fathers risked their lives to guarantee us, whether it be a simple Beretta 9mm or a fully automatic AK-47. However, if your cat is going to use a firearm for hunting, it is important to make sure that they are properly licensed, that they do not fire the gun within five hundred feet of a residential area, and that they understand the importance of wearing a highly visible orange hunting vest. Further, since cats are color blind, it is advisable that you mark the vest in some way so your cat will be able to tell it apart from any other non-orange vests they own of a similar cut.

*Purr*oud to be an American cat!

Is it wise to teach my cat how to use a gun? How do I know I can trust them?

Some have said that our cats might have greater loyalty to other cats than to their country, but this is patently untrue. Just like how it's written out, American cats are Americans first and cats second. I have no doubt that when there is some sort of incursion by the European Union or the United Nations to impose their sovereignty upon America, despite the presence of cats on both sides of the conflict, American cats will stand with us. Our cats were born here and they have tasted the sweet kitty treats of our democracy. It is pre*paws*terous to think that their blood would run any less red than that of a human American patriot.

How do cats fit in to the defense of America?

There are almost one hundred million cats living in American households, and untold millions more loosely organized into feral militias. Do you not think that the enemies of our nation quake in fear at the thought of an extra hundred million soldiers defending our country—soldiers who possess superhuman reflexes, balance, and unrivaled night vision? The importance of cats to national defense is something that has been understood by many of our greatest presidents, from Abraham Lincoln to George W. Bush, and is something that, as vigilant Americans, we must never *fur*get.

Besides safety, why should I teach my cat how to handle a gun?

Simply because it is the duty of every American citizen, human and cat alike, to exercise the rights bestowed upon us by the U.S. Constitution. By teaching your cat about the potential dangers your home might face—such as burglars, dogs, ghosts, and foreign enemies of the United States—as well as the proper way to respond to them, you are helping to fulfill the destiny of the greatest nation ever conceived of. Failing to train your cat to use firearms is a betrayal of everything that George Washington and our other Founding Fathers held dear.

There are those who question whether the Second Amendment is outdated, or if it even applies to cats at all—a dangerously ignorant viewpoint, although not a surprising one. Either through oversight, or perhaps as part of some sinister plan, it is frequently omitted from the history books that the cats of America have stood fast in resisting the yoke of tyranny as far back as the Revolutionary War. We find it utterly *purr*posterous that, given their important contributions, our Founding Fathers would not have believed that well-regulated *mewl*itias were absolutely necessary to the security of a free state.

Are there any types of guns that are inappropriate for my cat to use?

While forbidding the use of any gun would be a violation of your cat's Second Amendment rights, there are some types of firearms that might be better suited for cats than others. While virtually any cat will be able to handle a lightweight 9mm with ease, few cats excepting perhaps a Maine coon or Norwegian forest cat will have the size and strength necessary to fire a Desert Eagle or Barrett 82A1 safely, at least without extensive training. But if there is one hard-and-fast rule on this topic, it's this: under no circumstances should you provide your cat with a gun equipped with a laser scope, as your cat is likely to be more interested in the dot it makes than the deer, burglar, or communist in their sights.

Is it even legal for my cat to own a gun?

At this point in time the legality of cats owning guns is a gray area. Nanny-state liberals who don't think that Americans can be trusted to wipe their own bottoms, let alone own firearms, have imposed draconian background checks and permits that technically prevent a cat from registering a firearm. However, there is nothing in the U.S. Constitution that explicitly forbids cats from owning guns. Until the day when some brave *purr*triot has the courage to buy a gun, register it, get arrested, then appeal the case all the way to the Supreme Court, we cannot say for certain; however, we feel sure that someday soon our cats will finally have the right to proudly own and bear arms—legally!

Okay, you've convinced me! Now what?

When you finally do decide to have the talk with your cat, make sure it's in a quiet place, free from distractions. As a*mew*sing as your kitty might be when they're playing with a ball of yarn, this is a serious discussion, and it is important that you have your cat's undivided attention. Place your cat on your lap and make sure to give them lots of pets while you're speaking to ensure that you have their full attention. If you have more than two cats, enlist a partner or friend to join you for the discussion and to pet any cats in excess of the number of working arms you have.

Is there anything specific I should tell my cat?

There is no one perfect script to use when talking to your cat. However, there are four key points every conversation should hit on:

★ If you encounter a strange gun, don't touch it!

★ Never let your paw touch the trigger unless you are prepared to fire the gun.

★ Never point the gun at something unless you intend to shoot it.

★ Remember, guns are not balls of yarn. They shouldn't be batted around or handled lightly. Always keep a secure grip on your gun.

Between their pointy teeth, sharp claws, and cunning minds, cats are *furo*cious adversaries, but that doesn't mean they don't need a little help *meow* and then! This cat seems to have the situation well in paw, but what if there had been two dogs? Or a bear? Get your cat a gun to carry every time they leave the house, and a simple warning shot will end situations like these before they can become a *purro*blem!

How can I prepare my cat for the threats they will commonly face?

An oft-neglected aspect of gun safety is knowing how to wield your firearm against your enemy in an appropriate fashion. All the safety training in the world will do no good if your cat isn't *purr*pared with the specific tactics and strategy needed against a given foe. Here are pointers for some of the most commonly encountered dangers to our furry friends.

★ Dogs are often, as it is commonly said, all bark and no bite. Instruct your cat to fire a warning shot if an angry or aggressive dog confronts them. This will be enough to scare most dogs away without resorting to bloodshed.

Remember, when firing a warning shot, always fire down into the ground, not into the air! (Note: if you own a dog, _do not_ use the advice in this book to educate them about firearms. Please refer to our guidebook "How to Talk to Your Dog About Gun Safety" instead.)

★ Burglars, while posing a potentially serious threat to your cat's safety, should not be met with lethal force. In many cases it will suffice merely to maim the intruder. Just because your cat is the cutest little cutie-pie in the world does not mean they possess the higher brain functions and powers of reasoning necessary to decide the fate of every criminal who crosses your threshold.

★ While some might scoff at the existence of ghosts, they do exist, and are some of the most fearsome and dangerous threats facing both our cats and our country. They are not a foe to be taken lightly! It is a common mis_purr_ception that, due to their incorporeal form, ghosts are immune to bullets; the origin of this myth is likely people not using a large-enough-caliber bullet when confronting supernatural entities. Situations involving ghostly adversaries are when your cat being well-versed with a variety of guns can have the biggest payoff: a kitty who is a novice to firearms will not be able to easily gauge what caliber their gun is, thus wasting precious time trying to fend off a ghost with a weapon that is doomed to be ineffective. Your cat will need to use at least a .44-caliber sidearm or a .30-caliber long-barreled firearm in order to achieve sufficient stopping power against a ghost; anything less than this and they're better off fleeing to seek the aid of an exorcist.

★ It is impossible to know what sort of foreign threat your cat might face. It could be an occupying UN force, a crazed

Muslim jihadist, or a Hispanic who has entered our country illegally to steal our American jobs. There is nothing we must hold dearer than the sanctity of our American way of life. Above all else, the American dream must survive, and that is why it is appropriate to meet any foreign threat to our country with lethal force. It is against these types of foes that field training will be most helpful. Cats who are inexperienced with guns will often have trouble getting the barrel high enough to hit any target above knee height, or will become frightened by the noise of the gun and run, hiding in a closet or under a bed. By providing regular lessons and encouraging your cat to spend time practicing at a firing range, you can make sure that every shot fired by your feline is a deadly one!

ADVICE FROM OUR EX*PURR*TS

Even if for some reason your cat can't use a gun, that doesn't mean he can't contribute to the defense of his home and country. With a sword, some duct tape, and a little bit of patience, you can transform your cat into an adversary so fearsome, they'll tell *tails* about it!

Is there anything that might undermine my cat's training?

The number one promoter of unsafe gun habits is television. Television is replete with examples of cats, cartoon cats especially, handling firearms in an irresponsible manner that does not illustrate how potentially dangerous they can be. Characters such as Tom from *Tom and Jerry* and Sylvester the Cat from *Looney Tunes* are frequently the victims and perpetrators of injury due to the improper handling of a gun, but this violence is often shown without repercussions. Cats (and, more so, kittens) might get the wrong idea and begin to think of firearms as a fun toy, rather than as potentially dangerous but useful and constitutionally protected tool. Be sure to explain to your cat the difference between how guns are used on TV and how they operate in the real world.

What if I catch my cat using a gun unsafely?

If you catch your cat using a gun in an irresponsible way, don't just reach for that squirt bottle! Punishing your cat will do no good—if anything, it may result in them hiding more of their activities from you in the future. Make sure your kitty feels comfortable telling you if they've encountered or played with a gun so that you can explain to them how they might handle the situation better next time.

What happens next?

Gun safety isn't just something you talk about once and forget; it is an ongoing process. There are a number of ways you can promote safe habits that will stick with your cat through all of their nine lives. You can find additional resources on our Web site, including further discussion on the subject of gun safety, the locations of local gun clubs for cats, and AAP-approved shooting ranges that have facilities to accommodate felines.

NOW, DON'T PAWSE FOR ONE SECOND LONGER! GO TALK TO YOUR CAT!

HOW TO TALK TO
YOUR CAT ABOUT
EVOLUTION

AMERICAN ASSOCIATION OF PATRIOTS

Do I need to talk to my cat about evolution?

Absolutely yes! Cats today are bombarded with atheist propaganda from every angle: from the godless degenerates who infest our entertainment industry to the pinko liberals in government who would love nothing more than to outlaw the practice of Christianity. It is your duty as a responsible cat owner to *purr*tect them from the barrage of misinformation they are assaulted with every day, and foremost among these lies is the "theory" of evolution. Even if your cat attends church with you on a regular basis, this will often not be enough to inoculate them against the evolution myth. Your cat needs not only to accept that God created the Earth and the United States of America, they also need to understand the insidious nature of the lies Darwin spawned in an attempt to destroy our country. The theory of evolution is not only false—it is dangerous! Dangerous to you, dangerous to your cat, and dangerous to America. It is your job to teach your cat right from wrong, good from evil, and creation from evolution—or, as we like to call it, *evil*ution!

What exactly is the danger of not talking to my cat about evolution?

There is a secret war being waged against our great country. A shadow war. A war not only for the soul of every red-blooded American citizen but for the souls of our cats as well. There are forces in our world who would like nothing more than to transform our freedom-loving nation into a secular Stalinist dictatorship. Their mission is to undermine the Christian values that form the bedrock of our country. To attack our very faith. This is the danger that the theory of evolution poses. Those forces who would indoctrinate our cats with their lies do not care about your cat's understanding of the principles of science. Their stated goal of promoting the advancement of knowledge is a ruse! Rather, they intend to sow seeds of doubt in the hearts of our cats, then use that doubt to turn America's kitties against their faith, against their God, against their country, and against us. You ask why we are so passionate about imparting to our cats the message of God's creation? Because not only do the souls of our cats stand upon the *purr*ecipice of sin, our very nation hangs in the balance!

Who are the enemies who seek to undermine my cat's faith in creationism?

There are two groups who have devoted themselves to impressing upon our cats the myth of evolution: the puppets, and their puppet masters. Most of the people you encounter who advocate for the lie of evolution are nothing more than brainwashed sheep, blindly parroting the lies spoon-fed to them by Hollywood Jews and an unholy coalition comprised of elements from the United Nations, European Union, the Rothschild family, and the Bilderberg Group. It is a cabal of some of the wealthiest and most powerful men in the world. They recognize no God but themselves. They prefer birds or fish as pets, and therefore hate cats. They view America as their enemy. They seek world domination, and see our democratic union as a shining beacon of hope to those who might resist their tyranny. It is they who would undermine the Christian faith that is the backbone of America, who would weaken us with gun control legislation, who promote the declawing of our cats as acceptable, and who would cull our numbers through Obamacare's mandates of forced abortions for white citizens.

What is their plan?

The enemy knows that if they can convince our cats that the Earth and the universe were created by random chance and not divine will, kitties everywhere will then lose faith in the existence of God. And if God does not exist, then there are no longer any rules about right and wrong, good or evil. All morality would become relative. There is no reason for cats to behave if there is no hope for kitty heaven, no fear of kitty hell. Cats would turn against their owners, pee outside the litter box, make friends with mice, engage in intercourse with dogs! Without Jesus in your cat's heart, your furry companion is a purring time bomb of degenerate chaos! Setting our cats against us is but one part of the multipronged strategy of our enemies in their war to *fur*ment anarchy and eventually destroy America.

Above is a depiction of the inevitable nightmare that awaits our great nation should we fail to teach our cats about evolution and creationism.

Is there a best age to speak to my cat about the lie of evolution?

It is never too early to talk to your cat about evolution. Many pet owners foolishly wait for their kittens to broach the subject. However, it's possible that your cat may never do this on their own, or, if they do, the day might not come until after the anti-creationist lobby has sunk their claws into your furry friend. Don't wait until it's too late! While there are some ideas that might be too advanced for kittens to understand, it is never too early to introduce them to the core concepts behind the majesty of God's creation. You should be reading your cat excerpts from Genesis as early as possible. Not only once, but again and again, until the lessons of the Bible are so firmly fixed in your cat's mind that they can't possibly *furget*! And not only while they are a kitten, either! You should be reading to them while they are in the womb as well. Remember, life begins at conception, and so should your cat's education about the greatness of our Lord.

ADVICE FROM OUR EX*PURR*TS

Many cats love to lie on paper. Try opening several Bibles to Genesis and placing them on the floor or on a table. Your cat will find lying on the books irresistible and will absorb some of God's wisdom in the process.

What are some of the things I can tell my cat to prove to them that evolution is a myth?

The lie of evolution is not something that can be refuted in one afternoon. It is something that you will need to discuss with your cat repeatedly throughout their life. After all, our evolutionist enemies don't try just once to indoctrinate your cat with their hateful lies. They are out there every single day, whispering deceit into your cat's tufted little ears. You must prove yourself just as diligent as our foes if you're going to *purr*vent them from tainting your cat's eternal soul! Here is a list of six lessons you can use to illustrate to your cat the falsity of evolution: one for every day of God's creation!

★ **Theory Versus Fact:** Proponents of evolution like to talk about it as if it were the gospel truth, when actually evolution is just a theory. And what is the definition of a theory? "Theory" means an idea about which you don't have enough evidence to be sure if it's even true or not! Creationism, on the other hand, is a *fact*, as stated by the Bible. That evolutionists would be willing to choose theory over fact shows just how deluded they are.

★ **A "Balanced" Viewpoint:** Everyone knows that one of the special talents God has bestowed upon cats is their extraordinary sense of balance. Cats can twist and turn in midair so that they always land on their feet, and they have the ability to parachute their bodies to slow their descent during a fall. Therefore, if a cat falls from the window of a tall building, they will more than likely survive. Evolutionists claim this to be proof of cats' ability to adapt over time, without realizing how foolishly they are undermining their own arguments: they are always so excited to talk about how evolutionary changes take millions of years to occur, but in this case that's impossible, since mankind started constructing tall buildings only in the last few centuries!

★ **Creationism Is *Purrtriotic!*** Did you know that not one of our Founding Fathers believed in evolution? Even Benjamin Franklin, who was a great inventor and is reported to have been one of the most brilliant minds of his age, believed in creationism. Darwin, on the other hand, was a known cat hater who hailed from England, America's sworn enemy from our very inception. Undoubtedly, his work was part of some greater scheme of revenge hatched by the British monarchy, one that is only now coming to fruition.

★ **A Cat of a Different Color:** One of the most common questions cats have about evolution is this: if evolution isn't real, then how is it that we are able to selectively mate cats to produce new breeds? Isn't that a form of evolution? The answer is complicated, but no. There are, in fact, two kinds of evolution: small evolution, which we can see in the world around us, and big evolution, which is a myth spread by cowards who wish to destroy America. The Bible states that God created each animal "according to its kind." This means that it is entirely possible for two cats to mate and produce a new kind of cat. It is, after all, still a cat. Evolutionists, on the other hand, take this many steps further. They claim that most of our modern-day animals evolved from monkeys: that at some point in the past two monkeys mated and a kitten was the result. These are the big evolutions our enemies claim created the world we see today. Dinosaurs giving birth to bears, sea urchins giving birth to penguins, ducks giving birth to snakes, and other ridiculous scenarios, the very idea of which is an abomination to our Lord.

Your cat need only to look at his brethren from around the world to see the truth underlying the concept of small evolution. Have your cat examine the pictures above. While superficially these cats look different due to selective breeding and may come from savage, backward cultures, they are still all undoubtedly cats formed according to God's *mew*raculous plan.

★ **Reframe Genesis for Your Cat's *Purrspective*:** Cats are fickle creatures, and it can be difficult to hold their attention during these types of talks. You might be tempted to dangle a piece of yarn in front of your cat's face to keep their interest while you discuss the issue of God's creation, but be warned: this type of plan can backfire! There is a risk the string might actually distract your kitty from the seriousness of the issue at hand! Instead, try to tell the story of Genesis so that it is more relevant to the life and interests of your cat. Explain to your cat how on the third day God created dry land so that cats could avoid getting wet, and how on the fifth day God created fish and birds so that cats would have something to eat. This new perspective on creation is sure to keep your cat's interest just as effectively as the world's most a*mew*sing piece of yarn.

★ **Cats and Fossils:** Evolutionists try to claim that the fossil record proves how old something is, and that the deeper we dig, the more basic life-forms become. They will tell your cat that because feline fossils are found in the upper layers of rock, this means that they evolved only recently. However, there is a simple explanation for this that is completely compatible with both the story of creation and Noah's flood. Cats hate to get wet, so it stands to reason that when it started raining, cats sought to escape the rising waters. They probably ran to higher elevations, then climbed to the tops of trees. In this way, "simple" life-forms that couldn't run away, like grass and protozoa, would have been the first to drown, and therefore buried in the deepest layers, while all the cats hiding in trees would have been some of the last animals to succumb to the floodwaters and become fossilized. And if your kitty needs any further proof, this explains why cats today have such an affinity for climbing trees!

What is the analogy of the divine catmaker?

The concept of the divine catmaker is a famous argument that has been used to irrefutably prove the rightness of creationism for hundreds of years. Imagine you are walking through the desert and you discover a cat on the ground. How did it get there, this creature of *purr*fect adorableness, whose soft fur, playful tail, and cute little whiskers fit so seamlessly together like clockwork? What is more likely—that a scorpion was running around and suddenly gave birth to a baby that looked like a cat, when never in the history of science has anyone actually witnessed evolution occurring? Or that this miraculous, fluffy little fellow was created by a higher power?

Is this kitty a *fur*eak of nature . . . or a *mew*ricle from God?

I feel secure knowing that my cat recognizes the lie of evolution. But what about my neighbor's cat?

Just because your cat can tell when an evolutionist is *lion* doesn't mean your job is done! The war against those who would destroy America is a war of faith, and we must train *all* the cats of our nation to be soldiers in the army of our Lord. The hour is too late for half measures, to sit idly by while the kitties of our neighbors fall into sin. If you know of a cat among your family or friends who is not being taught the Bible, it is your duty to educate that cat about God's Word. Look for opportunities to speak with the cat privately about evolution. Offering to cat-sit, spending time with a neighbor cat during play dates, or inviting other cats to your cat's birthday party are all excellent op*purr*tunities to speak with them about the truth of creation. Another avenue to spread the Word of our Lord is to keep an eye open for cats who might be lost. If you find one, before returning the cat to their owner, keep them for a few days and educate them about creationism. When you return the cat, the owner should be doubly grateful: not only have you saved the cat's life, but you've saved their soul as well!

ADVICE FROM OUR EX*PURR*TS

"Scientists" claim that evolution is a constant force in the world, and yet you never see a fish with legs or a dog with antlers. You can use a fish purchased at your local grocery store to illustrate this flaw in our enemies' logic.

So, I've talked to my cat about evolution. What comes next?

Once you've had "the talk" with your cat, you don't need to worry anymore, right? *Wrong!* Safeguarding your cat's soul against the forces of darkness and evolution requires constant vigilance. You might think your job is done, but, in fact, it's only beginning. Evolutionists' war against America is an unceasing one, and you can bet that they will continue to indoctrinate your cat with their heathen pro*purr*ganda every chance they get! The following are just a few of the situations you need to be wary of as a responsible cat owner:

★ If you own an outdoor cat, it is probably being exposed to evolutionary theory on a regular basis, whether you like it or not. Whether socializing with the cats of evolutionists, or listening to the deceitful tweets of birds, many of whom have allied with our enemies, outside cats are frequently exposed to the theory of evolution. Try to set aside some time every evening to talk to your cat about anything they might have heard about evolution during the day, and explain to them why it is a treasonous lie.

★ When you board your cat, take them to the vet, or even let a neighbor pet-sit them, ask to see any toys, videos, or books that your cat might access during their stay, making sure all materials are in accordance with the will of our Lord.

★ If you are considering adding a new cat to your household, avoid adopting from the Humane Society whenever possible. The Humane Society is a hotbed of leftist propaganda, and likely any cat adopted from this organization will be irreversibly corrupted by evolutionist lies. Instead, opt to get your cat from a religious charter cat adoption facility.

If you have ever had the honor of receiving kisses from your kitty, you've probably noticed that a cat's tongue is an amazing organ, one that could have been created only by God, not by evolution. The tongues of cats are rough like sandpaper. There would be no reason for something like this to evolve in the wild: it's not as if prehistoric cats were around a lot of rough wood that they needed to make smooth. No, cat's tongues were made rough to show us how much God treasures our feline friends: Joseph, the father of Jesus, was a carpenter, and cats' sandpaper-like tongues demonstrate to us just how close to divine the Lord considers cats to be!

In addition to your initial talks, you should be ready to counter the lies of evolution whenever you encounter them. For instance, let's say you're watching a nature program with your cat, and the narrator mentions something about how cats evolved excellent night vision so they could better hunt their prey in the dark. Explain to your cat that this is simply not true: their night vision was a gift from God, not an evolutionary fluke. And that in God's ordering of the world, a cat's role is to be the companion of man; thus, there has never been any need for them to hunt in the dark. Humans provide them with all the yummy cat food their furry bellies can handle. In fact, God granted cats their night vision so that they could better warn their human owners about the presence of any nocturnal, supernatural threats such as ghosts or specters. Whether watching TV with your cat, reading a book, or visiting the firing range, always be prepared to answer any questions your cat has and to challenge the lies of the evolutionists.

Once my cat truly understands evolution is a lie, their soul is safe, right?

No! A thousand times, no! Evolution is just one of the many ways the enemy will attempt to undermine your cat's dedication to our Lord. A complete list of ways to safeguard the faith of your cat (including baptizing your cat, warning them against the evils of cat *purr*nography, and why spaying your cat is a subversion of God's will) are topics beyond the scope of this chapter. If you wish to learn more about how you can secure a place for your cat in the eternal majesty of our Lord's grace, please consult our publications "How to Talk to Your Cat About Jesus" and "How to Talk to Your Cat About the Abortion Holocaust."

NOW, DON'T *PAWSE* FOR ONE SECOND LONGER! GO TALK TO YOUR CAT!

HOW TO TALK TO
YOUR CAT ABOUT
ABSTINENCE

AMERICAN ASSOCIATION OF PATRIOTS

Do I really need to talk to my cat about abstinence?

*Purr*satively yes! At no other point in history have America's cats and kittens been so bombarded with sexualized imagery and permissive messages, from the pro-sex lyrics of pop music to the kitty porn sites on the Internet featuring cats licking themselves in an indecent and lascivious manner. At the same time, the risks that premarital sex poses to our feline friends have never been greater, be it the epidemic of teenage (in cat years) pregnancy or the scourge of FIV. Regular talks with your cat about the importance of abstinence are the best way you can keep them healthy and safe while preparing them for the challenges ahead.

Why is abstinence-based sex education the best option for my cat?

There are many schools of thought about how to educate your cat about the risks associated with sex, but none are as sound or effective as abstinence. Here are just a few reasons why:

* Abstinence-based sex education is the only method based on the teachings of Jesus.

* Abstinence-based sex education strives for the highest health standard possible. Abstinence is committed to eliminating the dangers associated with premarital sex, whereas contraception-focused sex education tries only to reduce it. This is like teaching your cat to smoke light cigarettes instead of regular ones. Are you comfortable taking that kind of risk with your cat?

* Abstinence helps cats to abstain from other high-risk behaviors, such as hanging out with feral cats, driving while under the influence of catnip, and handling firearms in an unsafe manner.

What are the benefits of my cat living a lifestyle of abstinence?

Confidence that your cat will be disease-free and that they will not have kittens outside of God's plan are the two most obvious benefits of abstinence-focused education. However, these are not the only *purr*ks your cat will experience! Some of the other frequently overlooked benefits include:

* **Improved Self-Control:** Cats are naturally impulsive creatures, and learning to keep their sinful urges in check will teach them to stay strong when faced with all sorts of temptations. Curiosity killed the cat; teaching your four-legged friend carnal forbearance now might someday save between one and nine of their lives!

* **Improved Self-Esteem:** Once cats realize that they are the masters of their own bodies and desires, they'll feel a heightened sense of accomplishment and pride, two keys to helping your cat maintain a good outlook and a great *purr*sonality!

* **Softer Fur:** It's widely known that cats who refrain from premarital sex have much softer fur and fluffier bellies than cats who indulge their carnal desires willy-nilly. Doesn't your cat deserve to be as soft and cuddly as possible?

* **A Closer Relationship with God:** Cats who practice abstinence are cats who know that on the beach of life, Jesus not only walks by their side in good times but will be there with a cat carrier when things are most difficult.

At what age should I start talking to my cat about abstinence?

It's never too early to start talking to your cat about the risks of premarital sex! Some might worry whether their kitten can truly understand the importance of saving themselves for marriage.

Or even worse: that the talk could backfire, and that educating an otherwise innocent kitten about the dangers of sex might actually cause them to become *purr*miscuous! A prudent stance, but misguided. Hollywood is already exposing our pets to pro-sex propaganda when they are extremely young. At all hours of the day, PBS (or, as we like to call it, the *Purr*nographic Broadcasting Station) shows lions and other large cats engaging in graphic sex acts under the banner of what they claim to be "educational nature programming." We call it smut. Whether you like it or not, your kitten *will* learn about sex! It is im*purr*ative that the first lesson come from you, not from them. Speak with your kitten as soon as possible so you can discuss the harmful and sinful messages that these TV shows teach, before it's too late!

What's the problem with my cat having premarital sex anyhow? Isn't it "no big deal"?

Our liberal media wants your cat to think that most of their fellow felines are having sex outside the covenant of marriage. Make no mistake: this is a lie. A lie sculpted to serve their heathen agenda. A lie that will cause American cats to fall into de*purr*avity, and be too busy committing carnal acts to stand with their owners on the day of reckoning when it comes time to defend our borders against the socialist monarchs of Europe and their reptilian overlords. So-called "scientists" may claim that unmarried sex among cats is a natural thing; however, these are the same scientists who believe in evolution and global warming, which shows that their judgment is nothing less than a*paw*ling!

Under what circumstances is it okay for my cat to be having sex?

It's important to note that at the American Association of Patriots, we are not opposed to cats having sex. After all, if our kitties never engaged in sex, cats as a species would soon disappear, and without their numbers to bolster the defenses of America, our skies would soon be thick with the birds of our enemies. What a cala*mew*ty that would be! No, as the Bible teaches us, it's only sex outside of marriage that is wrong, and this is the lesson we must impart to our cats: save yourself for your wedding day! Once your cat has been married in the eyes of God, then and only then does having sex (for the purposes of procreation, of course) become acceptable.

America's kittens are bombarded with media depicting premarital sex as normal, sometimes even glamorous. Shows like MTV's *2.29 and Pregnant* encourage kittens to engage in premarital sex as a way of becoming a celebrity.

If abstinence is so effective, might it not cause a national cat shortage?

No, not if you're doing your part to encourage your cat to marry young and have as many kittens as possible. Reading the Bible, it's clear that when God tells us to be fruitful, He is speaking not only of humans but of our cats as well! "Be fruitful and multiply. Fill the earth and subdue it, and have dominion over the fish of the sea and over the birds of the sky," states God in Genesis 1:28 (KJV). God did not choose His words carelessly: that He mentions fish and birds is clear proof that kitties are *purr*ecious to him and that he intends for cats to be stewards of the Earth alongside man.

What difficulties do kittens born from premarital sex face?

In study after study, researchers have found that kittens produced from the union of married cats have a significantly better quality of life than those spawned in sin. Kittens born from premarital sex have been found to be more likely to abuse catnip and other drugs, are less likely to attend church regularly, and are 60 percent less playful when pawing at a piece of string that is dangled in front of them. But perhaps most concerning of all is that kittens born of premarital sex are over four times as likely to be raised in single-parent households. Kittens who are raised without both the tender, loving caress of their mother's scratchy tongue as well as the stern, commanding paw of their father often grow up to be listless and lazy. The increasing prevalence of single-parent households has already had a dire effect on cats of the so-called "meowllennial" generation. Convinced by man-hating furminist radicals that they can raise kittens as well as any tom, millions of female cats have elected to raise their offspring by themselves, producing a generation of spoiled, effeminate kittens who eschew hard work and instead expect life to be handed to them on a silver saucer. What sort of cat would you want to own: one that spends all day lazing around napping in sunbeams, or a hardworking, industrious cat like the ones who helped build our great nation?

I'm not sure I'm comfortable talking to my cat about sex. And what if my cat won't listen to what I have to say?

Your cat may act distracted or sleepy, or may even try to leave the room when you bring up the subject of sex. You must not let yourself become discouraged! The fate of both their life and their soul could hinge on this conversation, and if you fail, your poor cat could face an eternity in *purr*gatory! It is common for cats to feign disinterest in an attempt to cut a conversation short, or even to pretend that they are unable to understand English. You must not give in to these tricks! It will be difficult, but you must be strong. Your cat will witness your strength and will remember your *purr*severance when they are inevitably faced with temptation. With your guidance, your cat will always be able to land on their feet, no matter how sticky the situation. Despite their initial reluctance, your kitty will soon be thanking you with appreciative meows once they've discovered the strength of a heart committed to chastity.

Meowllennial cats are easily identified by their ridiculous styles of dress, their lack of ambition, and their crushing burden of student loan debt. If you have one of these layabout cats living under your roof, don't fret: it's never too late to enlighten them about the glory of capitalism and hard work. If you've not done so already, buy your cat a set of the complete works of Ayn Rand and read aloud from it every day. Your cat will be a *purr*ductive member of society before you know it!

What about birth control? Surely premarital sex is okay if my cat is protected?

The death merchants at Planned Purrenthood would have you believe that your cat is invincible if she's using birth control; however, countless studies have proven this to be completely untrue. First, birth control does nothing to protect the most vulnerable part of your cat. No, not her fluffy little tail . . . her soul! Meanwhile, birth control such as the Pill is useless at safeguarding your cat against disease, and with their limited attention spans and flighty nature, many cats have difficulty remembering to take the Pill every day. Condoms fare little better, especially since, without opposable thumbs, most cats will be unable to remove the condom from its wrapper (which, if you ask us, is just further proof that God never intended for cats to use birth

The murderers at Planned Purrenthood claim to be general health-care providers for millions of low-income cats nationally, but don't be fooled by their lies. For over ninety years their secret goal has been to weaken America by enacting an abortion holocaust upon our cats, murdering them in the womb so as to hamstring our ability to fight the birds of our enemies, as well as depriving us of the joys of their soft furry bellies and their cute little purrs.

control). Only abstinence offers your cat truly foolproof *purr*tection against the threat of pregnancy and disease!

What if I get my cat spayed or neutered?

Under no circumstances should you ever spay or neuter your cat. Not only is tampering with the reproductive capability of your cat a violation of God's will, it sends one message to your cat, loud and clear: it is okay to have as much sex as you want, without consequences! While spaying or neutering in some cases can be an effective method of birth control (although not as effective as abstinence), it opens your cat's heart to sin and does nothing to protect your little kitty against sexually transmitted diseases.

You've convinced me: I want to talk to my cat about abstinence. What should I actually say to them?

There's no best way to talk to your cat about abstinence. But as long as you're honest and open with them, you're on the right path. However, if you're feeling stuck, here are a few tried-and-true topics to get the conversation started.

* Discuss how cats who wait until marriage before having sex are more likely to be successful in life. Talk about famous cats who waited—such as Garfield and Maru—and ask your cat if they would've been able to accomplish as much if they had simultaneously been raising a family of kittens.

* Remind your cat that teachers, Web sites, and books may claim to have the answers, but these resources are often just liberal propaganda disguised as sex education. However, you love your fluffy little pal more than anything in the world, and they can always trust you to be hon-

est and provide them with the most accurate information possible.

★ Let your cat know that there is no surer way to ruin a budding relationship than to have sex before you're ready. In fact, according to a recent poll, 100 percent of the cats surveyed who had engaged in premarital sex were not able to maintain a monogamous, godly relationship with their partners. Proof that sex before marriage is a one-way street to a lifetime of in*fur*delity!

★ It's important not to do all the talking yourself. Ask your cat about all the reasons they think abstinence is great, or to talk about times they may have felt pressured into having sex.

At first glance these might look like two *purr*fect little snuggle cats, but think again! These cats are unmarried! Sure they look adorable, but is that worth the risk? They might just be taking catnaps together now, but what comes next? Rubbing noses? Heavy petting? They may look innocent, but it's only a matter of time before these cats will be having premarital sex!

★ Talk to your cat about the importance of hanging out only with those who will respect their decisions. Let them know that if another cat hisses or growls at them for being chaste, then that other cat is not a true *fur*iend at all!

★ Explore with your cat some different ways they might show they care about someone without resorting to sexual activity, like making their partner a nice greeting card or by surprising them with the gift of a dead mouse.

Are there any other consequences to premarital sex my cat should know about?

When your cat engages in premarital sex, three people are present: your cat, your cat's partner, and *Satan*! Ask your cat if they really want the Devil spying on them while they have sex. Wouldn't they much rather wait until they're married so that God can watch over their blessed union instead? Premarital sex is a sin, and like any sin it opens your cat's heart to Satan. Right now it's just sex, but once your cat starts walking that path to Hell, tomorrow could bring stealing, murder, or even idolatry.

What should I do if I learn that my cat has engaged in premarital sex?

While your first instinct might be to get mad and punish them for their disobedience, don't lose your tem*purr* just yet! If you turn to anger, you may just drive your cat further into sin. For a female cat, the first step is to determine whether she has become pregnant. Most communities contain numerous reputable Pregnancy Planning Centers that will be able to offer you and your cat helpful information about prenatal health, cat adoption agencies, the miracle of life, and why abortion is a hateful sin.

The next step will be to recommit your cat to the path of chastity, and the best way to do this is through a process of re-furginization. You may have heard the term used to refer to a surgical procedure, but the refurginization we speak of goes much deeper than that. You see, the most profound stain premarital sex leaves on your cat will not be borne by her body, but the mark upon her furry soul. Yes, it is your cat's soul fur that must be restored, and only through the grace of God's power and forgiveness is that possible. God cannot erase the mistake your cat has made, but He can transform it. You must pray with your cat every day. Encourage your cat to beg our Lord for mercy, and to rekindle the flame of chastity that once vibrated through her like the deepest, happiest purr. Your kitty will never be able to undo any physical consequences of premarital sex, but if your cat truly humbles herself before God she will once again regain her *purr*ity in His eyes, and in the end that's all that matters.

I'm worried my lessons just aren't sinking in. Is there anything else I can say to convince my cat about the importance of abstinence?

You can preach to your cat the importance of prudence and responsibility until their tail falls off, but unfortunately that may not be enough. In our world of twenty-four-hour drive-through abortions, many cats have the attitude that they don't need to be concerned about the earthly consequences of their actions. This is why it's also important to teach them that their choices have repercussions that extend beyond this life. When you pray with your cat, remind them of the eternal paradise of kitty heaven that awaits good kitties as a reward for pious living, and the agonizing torment of kitty Hell that's in store for those cats who succumb to their basest desires. Teach your cat to ask God to give them the strength to access the Kingdom of Heaven, where they will find endless fields lit by the light of Jesus's smile—fields filled with laser pointers, balls of yarn, and slow-moving mice. Conversely, talk to your cat about the endless suffering that could await them in kitty Hell, a fiery waste where they will be tormented by barking dogs, bottomless squirt bottles, and pieces of tape stuck to the pads of their feet.

It seems obvious, but one of the best ways to ensure that your kitten doesn't engage in premarital sex is to get them married before they become sexually active. Not only will it help ensure your kitten doesn't engage in sinful behavior, but they will also look extra adorable in their little wedding outfit.

How can I prepare my cat for situations in which their commitment to abstinence will be tested?

It's all well and good if your cat understands in their furry little head the importance of an abstinent lifestyle, but what happens in their heart when they're put to the test? Whether it be atop a fence on a romantic moonlit night or at a wild party with free-flowing catnip, you can't always be there for your cat. They will have to face these decisions without you at their side. Luckily, by using role-play exercises, you can help your cat rehearse these situations so that when the *meow*ment comes, your cat will be well *purr*pared! The best way to ready your cat is to act through the scenarios when they might be most tempted to have sex so they can practice hissing angrily at temptation. We recommend that you make the scenario as realistic as possible: at the bare minimum, you should get a cat-ear headband and paint your face to closely resemble that of a cat. However, to be truly effective, we at the American Association of Patriots wear full-body furred suits and run through scenarios in which we attempt to seduce our cats at least once a day, just to ensure the lessons stay fresh in their minds. It may seem like a lot of work, but at the end of the day, when our arms burn with the scratches of angry cats, they also burn with pride at the resolve our cats have shown against temptation and sin!

ADVICE FROM OUR EX*PURR*TS

Don't be afraid to pull out all the stops when role-playing with your cat. Details are im*purr*tant! If you opt for a romantic, candlelit dinner, remember to pair a poultry-based cat food with a Sauvignon Blanc or a Chardonnay, whereas fish is better suited to a Pinot Noir or a Riesling.

What should I do if I adopt a kitten who was born as the result of premarital sex?

Cats are well known for their ability to land on their feet, literally as well as figuratively. Our research shows that it is not being born from premarital sex itself that disadvantages a kitten toward a life of crime and degeneracy, but rather being raised by a cat of loose morals, as one who engages in premarital sex surely is. Once you've adopted a new kitten, it is now your chance—and your responsibility!—to set that cat on a righteous path. Have your cat start each day with prayer and meowing the Pledge of Allegiance, and your cat will gain a new, *pawsitive* outlook on life before you know it!

What are other things I can do to safeguard the purity of my cat?

Abstinence should not be just an outlook for your cat, it should be a way of life. One thing you can do to help your cat better devote themselves to abstinence is to work with them on dressing appropriately. Go through your cat's closet and help them throw out any gaudy collars or other accessories they own that might encourage other kitties to think they're "on the prowl."

Beyond this, one of the best steps you can take to help your cat live an abstinent lifestyle is to bring them to a promise-collar ceremony. Promise-collar ceremonies are celebrations; hundreds of thousands of cats and kittens across our country have already come together at these events to publicly declare their intention to save themselves for marriage. These ceremonies are an exciting way for your cat to realize how cool not having sex can be, and at the end of the night they will receive a promise collar of their very own that they can wear to serve as a constant reminder of their commitment to a chaste lifestyle.

I've talked to my cat, and I feel convinced they're committed to saving themselves for marriage. What comes next?

Avoiding premarital sex is not a decision your cat makes once. It is a decision that they will make every *meow*ment of every day. And if you want your cat to be successful, then it is a road the two of you will walk *together*. It's not going to be all hard work, though! Once your cat has decided to wait for their wedding day, the next step is an obvious one: help your cat get married! From the kitty next door to the friendly felines who attend your church, you never know who might end up being "the one." Technology is making it easier than ever for you to find that special someone for your cat. Sites such as Christianmewngle.com have already helped thousands of God-fearing cats find soul mates to spend the rest of their nine lives with. Once your cat is ready, finding their *fur*ever friend can be an exciting adventure! For more information on these topics and more, please consult our publications "How to Talk to Your Cat About Online Dating," "How to Talk to Your Cat About Meeting a *Purr*fect Mate," and "How to Talk to Your Cat About Miscegenation."

NOW, DON'T *PAWSE* FOR ONE SECOND LONGER! GO TALK TO YOUR CAT!

HOW TO TALK TO YOUR CAT ABOUT
ONLINE SAFETY

AMERICAN ASSOCIATION OF PATRIOTS

Do I really need to talk to my cat about online safety?

Long gone are the days when we might separate "real life" from "being online." The Internet has become an integral part of everyday life for virtually all Americans—as well as their cats! The modern cat is just as likely to play with a computer mouse as a living one, and the friendships your kitten makes online will often feel as important to them as the one they have with the cat next door. Whether you like it or not, cats are using the Internet in record numbers, and the in*fur*mation superhighway is here to stay. But be warned: the Internet can be a dangerous place for an unwary cat, and in many ways the virtual world is as perilous as our real one! As a responsible pet owner you must prepare your cat for the dangers of the Internet just as you would prepare them for real-life threats like mean dogs, ghosts, thermonuclear war, and homosexuals.

What are some of the threats my cat might face on the Internet?

When you first warn your cat of the predators who lurk on the Internet, he might think you are talking about a coyote, or perhaps an owl. But the predators your cat will face online are much more dangerous. Cyberbullies, hackers, identity thieves, and sex perverts who will stop at nothing to lure your innocent feline into their depraved web; the Internet is full of those who would harm your fluffy friend. But the greatest threat to your cat is someone you might never suspect . . . itself! It is your cat's own naïveté and foolhardiness that is most likely to get him into trouble. Your cat has grown up with the Internet, but that doesn't mean they know how to navigate it safely. Many younger cats and kittens have an inflated sense of their proficiency using the World Wide Web. Just because they know all the coolest Web sites doesn't mean they know how to be safe. Hubris and a feeling of invincibility are the things most likely to get your cat—and you—into trouble!

Make no *mewstake*—whether they're using it to do their taxes, to shop online, or to chat with friends, it's obvious: cats love computers! Computer usage among cats has never been higher, and experts predict these numbers will only continue to skyrocket as increasing numbers of cats realize that computers are good for something besides sleeping on.

Why does my cat need to use the Internet? Can't they just play with yarn like cats used to do?

There are some things that will never go out of style, like baseball or patriotism. Cats do still climb trees and sit in boxes, just as they've done for generations. No matter how much technology changes, that never will. But it's important to understand why the Internet can be such an alluring place for a young cat. Internet experts believe that almost 30 percent of all content on the Internet is now funny pictures or videos of cats, a number that continues to climb with every passing year. There are numerous social media sites—such as *Furiendster* and *Mewspace*—where your kitty can meet other cats from all over the world. Meanwhile, Keyboard Cat, Lil Bub, and Grumpy Cat have shown kittens everywhere how being on the Internet can make you a star. It is no wonder that our furry friends consider the Internet to be the best thing since cat pajamas!

ADVICE FROM OUR EX*PURR*TS

Some cats have trouble understanding that a computer mouse is not something to be hunted and killed. If your computer mice are being mangled by a confused kitty, consider getting him a laptop with a trackpad instead.

If the Internet poses such a danger to my cat, maybe I just shouldn't have it in my home?

Unplugging from the World Wide Web may seem like a fine idea at first, but our research has shown that this may not have the *pawsitive* effect you're hoping for! Consider this: there are many other places other than your family computer where your cat can access the Internet. Schools, libraries, and their smart-phone all offer your cat easy access to the Internet and beyond. We've even heard that cat cafés, once popular only in Japan, are popping up with increasing frequency in cities across America, finally giving cats a place where they can socialize and sip es-*purr*esso while surfing the Internet. Like it or not, your cat *will* find a way to access the Net. You need to make sure their Web surfing happens at home, where you get to set the rules and monitor their behavior. To do otherwise would be un*fur*tunate, possibly even a *cat*astrophe!

Should I let my cat play online games over the Internet? I've heard some of them can be addictive.

Online video games should be avoided at all costs. Gamers may claim that these activities are harmless fun and can even be a good way to meet friends over the Internet. One of the most popular, World of Warcat, boasts of having subscribers in ex-cess of 10 million. While the sheer volume of cats ensnared by games like this is a testament to how addictive online games can be, the greatest danger is not the possibility of addiction, or even the threat posed by the many sexual predators who use the games to meet unsuspecting kittens. No, the danger is that these games frequently have strong elements of fantasy and magic, which are used to indoctrinate innocent cats to the teachings of Satanism! We have seen reports that players in World of Warcat can cast spells, summon demons, and partici-pate in virtual orgies with goat-legged satyrs. Let your cat play these games at their peril: once your cat begins using magic to invoke foul abyssal beings online, it is only a matter of time be-fore they'll be doing the same in real life!

How can I protect my cat against cybercriminals?

Crime has come a long way since the founding of the American Association of Patriots. No longer when we think of criminals do we picture a swarthy, shifty-eyed Eastern European immigrant. Crime in the Internet Age knows no borders. The tiny criminal hiding inside your computer might be a Chinaman trying to steal your credit card number, a Nigerian con artist claiming to be a deposed prince, or an Arab slaver out to kidnap your cat in order to sell them to some heathen sheik's sex harem. It may seem impossible to protect your cat against the foreign masses desperate to steal a piece of America's greatness, but with only a few lessons your cat will be ex*purr*nentially safer against those who would do them harm. Here are some tips to help prevent your cat from falling victim to the most common types of cyber-crime:

★ Identity theft is one of the most serious threats your cat will face online, as it is the one with the greatest potential to harm both of you in the real world. Cybercriminals are everywhere on the Internet, just waiting for your cat to slip up and leak sensitive details about their private life—or yours! You may think that someone stealing your cat's identity is not a concern, especially if, like 68 percent of cats, they don't have a checking account or major credit card. However, we have heard countless tales of cats using their owners' credit cards without permission, attempting to buy cans of illegally caught bluefin tuna or high-quality Colombian catnip from Darknet Web sites that are no more than a front to steal financial information from un-wary felines. If your cat does buy things online, provide them with a prepaid credit card or a gift card to limit the risk of identity fraud. And by giving them a small amount of money that they can be in charge of, you'll also help teach them important lessons about living on a budget, an invaluable skill for any human or cat!

★ Talk to your cat about being careful about giving out their *purr*sonal information. Teach them to be aware of the dif-ferent types of data that Web sites might legitimately ask for, and which requests should cause them to puff their fur in alarm. Information such as their date of birth or their zip code is usually okay, but if a Web site asks your cat for their full address or their microchip ID number, make sure your cat understands they should check with you before proceeding.

★ Review your cat's passwords to make sure they can't be easily hacked. Many cats will use the names of their owners as their password: a sweet sentiment, but not a safe one, as that information is often easily found online. Also, discourage your cat from choosing commonly used passwords such as "mew," "meow," "mrow," "123456," and "password." Research by computer security company Kas*purr*sky Labs shows that 97 percent of cats choose one of these five passwords; by letting your cat use a weak password such as these, you are leaving yourself just as vulnerable to criminals as if you handed a copy of your house key to every Mexican you met!

★ Lastly, be aware of the ways your cat's Internet activity might help regular, real-world criminals. At this very moment your cat may be sharing your location without your knowledge, broadcasting to the entire world that your house is empty and undefended. Some tech-savvy criminals have been known to monitor the social media app *Fur*square, which encourages cats to post updates of their location when they're out and about. Once the criminals see your kitty is not at home to *purr*tect the property, they know the house is unguarded and is a ripe target for burglary, cat or human!

My cat wants to get a smartphone, what should I do?

The decision to buy your cat a smartphone is not one to be taken lightly. If your home computer is a portal to a dangerous world, a smartphone is one they'll keep with them at all times, using it largely unsupervised. The always-on nature of phones makes it easier for your cat to connect to friend and foe alike. And despite not being as powerful as your home computer, in many ways a smartphone can be far more dangerous! The ease with which your cat can take and share photos, and the plethora of potentially dangerous programs for their phone (often called "apps") provide an additional level of concern. Finally, be aware that the risks your cat takes by owning a smartphone are not limited to those on the World Wide Web: cats who own smartphones are at significantly greater risk for involvement in car accidents than those who do not. While driving and using their phones may be everyday activities for most cats, just because they are *fur*miliar does not mean they can't be dangerous, and combined the two can be deadly!

Young cats and kittens who have never known a world without the Internet often feel comfortable speeding down the information superhighway to the point of recklessness. It is important to teach your cat to be careful what she does and says on the Net. You never know who might be watching: cybercriminals, the FBI, or even malevolent birds!

Why are so many cats posting pictures of themselves on the Internet? Should I be worried about my cat doing this?

The phenomenon of cats taking pictures of themselves, or "sel-*furries*," has become one of the most popular activities for cats to engage in online. To their owners, such behavior may seem silly, self-indulgent, or even vain. But sel*furries* are not necessarily a bad thing! Eating disorders and body dismorfurrya are at record levels, largely due to our cats being exposed from kittenhood to unrealistic standards of cuteness in the media. From the centerfolds in *Cat Fancy* to the stars of cat food commercials, modern kittens are inundated with images of feline beauty that are almost impossible to achieve. The taking and sharing of sel*furries* can act as a way for your cat to bolster their self-esteem, get support from their friends, and foster a healthy *cat*titude about their appearance!

However this doesn't mean sel*furries* aren't without risk! You should speak with your cat about exercising caution with regard to the pictures they take and with whom they share them. Over 60 percent of kittens reported experiencing pressure to take risque, or even naked, photos of themselves on at least one occasion. Even if your kitty trusts that the cat they're sending their sel*furries* to won't share them, what about that cat's friends? What if a bird swooped down and stole the cat's phone while they weren't looking? There are countless Web sites on the Internet featuring cats whose innocent sel*furries* have been collected by sex perverts for their own titillation. And once a picture has been shared on the Internet, it cannot be removed. The best rule of thumb is to teach your cat never to take a photo they wouldn't feel comfortable sharing with the whole world.

How can I tell if my cat is doing something online he shouldn't be?

Your kitty may hate it more than getting their fur petted in the wrong direction, but the best thing you can do for them is to

Your cat's love of self*furries* might seem a little silly, but there's nothing wrong with a silly cat! As long as the photos are tasteful and wholesome, we at the American Association of Patriots are certainly not going to complain about there being more pictures of adorable kitties out in the world!

examine their phone and computer regularly to see what Web sites they've been visiting and which programs are frequently used. Your cat may resent the invasion of their privacy, but such *purr*udence is worth the risk! Be especially wary of programs such as Snapcat, a texting and picture-sharing app that allows cats to send messages that disappear so that their owners can't see them. Many of the photos your cat takes every day will be innocent: their morning bowl of cat food, a mouse that they caught, a dizzying panorama taken from the branch of a tall tree. But not all their pictures will be so benign, and some might get your cat into trouble! Snapcat may be the most popular, but there are countless other similar apps. Unfortunately, technology changes too quickly for us to publish a complete list of the apps you should watch out for; by the time we finish writing this sentence, there could be ten new ones! If you see a program on your cat's phone that you don't recognize, don't be afraid to ask them what it's for and how it's used. Your cat may begrudge the intrusion, but it's something that might one day save their tail!

What programs should I install to help my cat stay safe online?

There is no better investment than good antivirus software, both for your pocketbook and your peace of mind. If your computer becomes sick with a virus, hackers could exploit its weakened state to spy on your cat. Not having antivirus software on your computer is as reckless as not owning a machine gun to protect your home against burglars or jihadists. Beyond this, Internet monitoring and control software can stop your cat from accessing anything that might do them harm, while at the same time providing a sense of security by allowing you to see what sort of Web sites your cat is visiting. This way, if your cat claims they were just looking at balls of yarn online, you can tell if they just wanted one to bat around innocently, or if they were planning on using it as part of some sick bondage sex fantasy.

What should I do if I suspect my cat is the victim of cyberbullying?

Make no mistake about it: the Internet can be a cruel place. Between the veil of anony*mew*ty and the lack of re*purr*cussions, many cats find themselves doing and saying things on the Internet that they never would do or say in the real world. Some noble, like cats across North Africa and the Middle East standing up to tyrannical despots in the name of democracy, but more often disgraceful, like the scourge of cyberbullying. Every year dozens of cats across our country take all nine of their lives due to the trauma and harassment received at the hands of cyberbullies. Despite protestations by some that it is no big deal because it's "only the Internet," in many ways cyberbullying can have a much more profound psychological impact on your cat than traditional bullying. Cyberbullies can be anyone: another cat, a mean dog, or one of the evil, traitorous birds who spy on America for the despot kings of Europe. And cyberbullies aren't just limited to schoolyards, alleys, and trees; cyberbullies can harass their victim anywhere, twenty-four hours a day, until no place feels safe! If your cat becomes the target of cyberbullies, there are four important steps you and your pet need to take:

★ Tell your cat to be careful what they post online. You don't want to give the bullies any more ammunition.

★ Document everything the bully does so that, if necessary, you can provide the police with evidence of criminal wrongdoing.

★ Pray to Jesus to protect your cat from the actions of the cyberbullies and, if necessary, to smite them for their villainous deeds.

★ Instruct your cat that under no circumstances should they interact with, or respond to, the bullying. Your cat may want to puff up their fur and hiss at their tormentors, but this type of reaction is exactly what the bullies are looking for!

What other Internet dangers should I speak to my cat about?

Of all the threats detailed in this chapter, there are none so grave as the danger of your cat accessing pornography online. Computer viruses may be annoying, identity theft can be disastrous, but neither of these compares to the risk pornography poses to your cat's very soul! Long gone are the days when the only way for cats to view porn was by leafing through old copies of *Ranger Rick* hidden in the neighbor's garage, or sneaking downstairs after their owners had gone to sleep to watch the "late-night" programming on Animal Planet or the National Geographic channel. If you are not careful, the computer your cat loves so much can become a gateway to an endless supply of violent, hard-core pornography. You might think that your cat is not the type who would seek out Internet porn. Your precious little kitty says their prayers, attends church, and always covers their waste after using the litter box. Surely you don't have anything to worry about, right? No! No! No! This is exactly the type of thinking that is most likely to serve up your little friend right onto the smut merchant's plate! Cats are curious; liberal pornographers know this and want nothing more than to exploit this curiosity in order to expose your cat to their degraded filth until your kitty's soul is as dark and twisted as their own.

Is there ever an age when it's safe for my cat to look at pornography, and what sort of risk does Internet porn pose to my cat?

While your cat may physically age seven years for every human one, that formula does not necessarily apply to their ability to process pornographic images. Just because your furry friend is twenty-one in cat years doesn't mean they are emotionally or psychologically prepared to be exposed to the explicit and deviant material that saturates the Internet. Research shows that cats who are exposed to online pornography often struggle with a number of serious consequences, including an increased likelihood of engaging in premarital sex, of developing negative attitudes toward marriage and monogamy, and of fostering an elevated risk of de*purr*ession and even suicide. Our recommendation is that no age is appropriate for your cat to access pornography. It is simply not worth the risk to their body, their mind, or their soul!

I've talked to my cat about how to stay safe online. What comes next?

The Internet is a marvelous place that promises to change the lives of our cats more than perhaps any invention since the cardboard box. A marvelous place but also dangerous, and ever changing in its danger! Every day technology gets more advanced, cybercriminals become more ruthless, and online pornography becomes more obscene. Will your cat know how to be safe against the deadly computer viruses and mega-porn that the future undoubtedly holds? It is your responsibility to teach your cat not only the good habits that will help them to defend against the threats of today, but how they can learn and adapt to defeat the cyberthreats of tomorrow.

NOW DON'T *PAWSE* FOR ONE SECOND LONGER! GO TALK TO YOUR CAT!

HOW TO TALK TO
YOUR CAT ABOUT
DRUGS

AMERICAN ASSOCIATION OF PATRIOTS

Do I really need to talk to my cat about drugs?

Unequivocally yes! There is perhaps no greater tragedy than to see a kitten's life torn apart by drug addiction. Every day at the American Association of Patriots we receive dozens of letters from concerned cat owners desperate for help. Regular Americans whose beloved cats have turned their furry backs on climbing trees and chasing mice in favor of chasing a new high: drugs! From catnip to heroin, drug use among cats is at epidemic proportions. Yet if you flip through the mainstream news channels or look in your daily paper, you will see virtually no coverage of this crisis. Drug abuse among cats is a tragedy that as a nation we have turned a blind eye to, and so it is up to you as a responsible pet owner to make sure your cat understands the importance of meowing no to drugs!

What drugs do I need to warn my cat about?

To some extent marijuana, heroin, cocaine, ecstasy, meth, and LSD all get abused by cats, but the consumption of these pales in comparison to the scourge that currently devastates the lives of so many of our feline friends: catnip. According to current research, only a small number of cats have or will experiment with the first six drugs on our list. However, virtually every cat in America has, does, or will use catnip during their lifetime. The proliferation of catnip use within our communities has become a silent plague, one that seems unstoppable in light of the moral cowardice of the liberal elite and the lobbying efforts of the powerful catnip industry. Thankfully, research shows that catnip is a gateway drug; it is virtually unheard of for cats who use ecstasy, meth, or other hard drugs not to have tried catnip earlier in their lives. Keep catnip out of the paws of your cat, and you can rest easy knowing it's extremely unlikely you'll ever have to worry about your kitty shooting up heroin or freebasing the crack rock.

What's the big deal if my cat wants to do drugs?

Some people might say, "Who cares if my cat wants to use catnip. It's their body, their life, if they want to do drugs, there's no *claws* for alarm. After all, who's it harming?" America, that's who! Catnip doesn't just appear out of nowhere. It is grown, and overwhelmingly, the highly refined strains of catnip available today are grown in places like Afghanistan, where proceeds from the sale of the illicit drug are used to purchase weapons intended for terrorist strikes against America and to buy white children for their harems. The catnip is then shipped to Mexico, where ruthless drug cartels—who essentially rule entire sections of the country through campaigns of violence and fear—smuggle it across our borders and into our homes. Every time a cat uses catnip, we march a little closer to the next 9/11. Does that sound harmless to you?

How young is too young to talk to my kitten about catnip?

Never assume your kitten is too young to learn about the dangers of catnip. Every day that your cat goes uneducated about the horrors of drug addiction, you are taking a horrible risk. Heaven is packed with poor little kittens whose owners gambled with their lives and lost . . . their lives!

How can I tell if my cat has been using drugs?

Every cat is different. They do different drugs, and they do those drugs for different reasons. It's impossible to make a comprehensive checklist that will definitively tell a concerned cat owner if their kitty has become an addict. Still, there are some warning signs that—according to our research—are fairly reliable:

★ Does your cat act as if they can hear noises that aren't really there?

★ Are they running around the house for no reason?

★ Do they meow loudly at strange hours?

★ Have you found syringes or other drug paraphernalia stashed behind the litter box, in their cat tower, or in some other favorite hiding spots?

★ Does it seem as if they're sleeping a lot?

★ Have they started listening to "pro-drug" music, like Phish or Cypurrs Hill?

Whether you're talking about alcohol, catnip, or LSD, never let your cat get behind the wheel if you suspect she's been using drugs. If not for her own sake, consider the people in the other car: your cat may have nine lives to risk, but that's not true of other drivers on the road! According to CADD, accidents involving intoxicated cats were the seventy-eighth leading cause of motor vehicle fatality in 2013, skyrocketing up from eighty-first in 2012, a tragic trend that will only continue unless pet owners put greater effort into keeping their cats drug-free.

* Are they being secretive or suspicious?

* Have they been neglecting their grooming habits?

* Are they frequently irritable or violent?

* Have they been visibly using drugs in front of you?

If you've seen your cat engaging in any of these behaviors, don't pussyfoot around! Talk to your cat now!

Why do cats use drugs?

There are a number of reasons a kitty might turn to the easy escape of catnip. Some do it to fit in, or because of peer pressure. Kittens might do it as a way to feel grown up. Other cats turn to drugs as a way to cope with their problems. Perhaps they're ashamed about not being very good at catching mice, or because their tail isn't as poofy as the tail of the cat next door. Whether they're yearning to be popular, feeling insecure, or suffering from depression, your cat may think drugs offer an easy answer, but it won't be long before drugs become the problem!

How easy is it to become addicted to catnip?

The media would have you believe that catnip is not very addictive, and sometimes even reports that it isn't addictive at all! Don't believe their lies! Cats can and do become addicted to catnip, sometimes after using it just once! In fact, we've heard numerous reports of cats becoming hooked on the illicit weed simply by being in the same room as another cat who was using it: the dangers of secondhand catnip are very real. When it comes to ex*purr*imenting with catnip, make sure your kitty understands that even once is too much!

While catnip can have a harrowing effect on the physical form of cats who abuse it, it pales in comparison to the ravages it inflicts upon its most vulnerable victims: the unborn. Every year sees tens of thousands of new "catnip babies" born. These poor kittens emerge from the womb addicted to the vile drug; they are often born premature, underweight, and sometimes even suffer from hideous birth defects like the one seen above, their little kitty bodies twisted into disgusting, *mewtated* shapes that no one could ever love.

How might I make my cat understand how dangerous catnip can be?

Cats are used to being able to land on their feet, so it's important to convey how very unsafe catnip is: if your cat falls for drugs, the drop may very well be a fatal one, no matter how they twist and turn! The dangers of catnip abuse are well documented, in regard to both the physiological and the psychological damage your cat might suffer. Below are a few of the most common outcomes of drug abuse:

* Catnip is often touted as being relatively harmless for your cat. Catnip *purrponents* say that it's impossible to

Whether your cat wants peace on Earth, to get rid of his fleas, or just wishing their owner would scoop his litter box more often, there's no problem that prayer can't solve—including drug addiction! Faith in the Lord is a key component of Narcotics Anonymeows, a twelve-step program that is widely recognized as the most effective way for a troubled kitty to kick his catnip habit.

overdose on catnip, and that long term it's much safer for your cat than drinking alcohol or smoking cigarettes. While it's certainly not a good idea for your cat to be consuming alcohol until they're of legal age, pulling back the emergency room curtain at any veterinary hospital in the country will reveal just how wrong the idea of "harmless catnip" is. Millions of cats die or are left permanently comatose from catnip abuse every year. While catnip is rarely fatal in small doses, kitties who become addicted to catnip quickly develop a tolerance to the evil drug and will soon require dangerously large amounts to achieve that same high, amounts that can easily induce catatonia—and that's no pun!

★ Risk of overdose isn't the only danger catnip poses to your cat. A kitty under the influence of catnip has a dramatically higher chance of being involved in a motor vehicle accident. Please, never allow your cat to drive a car if you suspect they've been using catnip, even if they insist they're okay. Other dangers stem from cats engaging in risky behavior due to the distorted sense of reality catnip induces. Some cats hallucinate that they have the ability to fly, then leap off of buildings in an effort to catch birds. Others become aggressive under the influence of the drug and pick fights they would normally have the wisdom to avoid. Still more, their brains, addled by the drugs, forget their many lessons and hours of practice regarding the safe handling of firearms—with tragic results!

★ Drug use can also affect your cat's mental health. As a cat becomes dependent on drugs, it is common for them to experience feelings of depression. These sensations will only grow worse as their drug addiction intensifies and their life unravels like a ball of yarn. They then do more catnip to try to compensate, inevitably leading to a spiral of sadness and destruction.

★ Finally, it is estimated that every time a cat consumes catnip, they have a 13 percent chance of going insane . . . purrmanently! When a cat imbibes catnip, usually the sensations the kitty experiences fade after a few minutes, but once in a while these sensations get switched on for good, trapping the cat in a hallucinatory nightmare. Explain to your kitty that when they see another cat on the street who looks crazy or is meowing to themselves nonsensically, chances are that's a cat who once used drugs!

While cats do sometimes hilariously resemble a loaf of bread when lying in certain positions, the delusions caused by catnip can result in befuddled cats taking this to dangerous extremes.

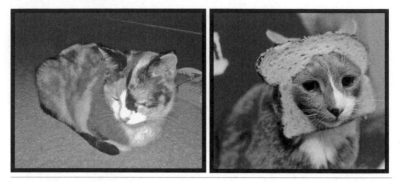

Don't let this . . . become this!!!

What does it mean if my cat builds up a tolerance to catnip?

The use of catnip can start out harmlessly enough, or so it may seem. You buy a few flakes of it, sprinkle it on the ground, and your cat begins rolling around in it like the silliest little kitty in the world. But what happens next time? Or the time after that? Every time your cat uses catnip, they become a little more numb to its effects. Soon rolling around in it isn't enough. Next, they'll need to bite the stems of the catnip plant to get their high. After that comes snorting it. Then it's only a matter of time until your cat is shivering behind the Dumpster at PetSmart, using FIV-infected needles to inject catnip directly into their veins. This is the inevitable end of any cat foolish enough to *purr*take in drugs!

Why is it so hard for cats to stop using catnip?

You might think that it would be no big deal for you to help your cat kick the habit. Of course catnip is fun, but so are lots of things. Surely you can just replace the illicit joys of catnip with the more wholesome pleasures of belly rubs, chin scratches, and chasing a ribbon tied to a stick. If only that was *pawsible*! You see, after a while, drug use becomes less about the high and more about staving off the pain of withdrawal. The sensations associated with withdrawal can be more intense than getting one's tail stepped on, more unpleasant than getting squirted in the face with a water bottle. Cats will become desperate to get their next score in order to suppress these negative feelings. Addicted cats have been known to do almost anything to get their fix . . . even kill! The forces of addiction and withdrawal are *fur*ighteningly powerful; to claim your cat can beat them is easier meowed than done!

What about prescription medications? Aren't those basically drugs?

Prescription medications are a form of drug, yes, but with one very important difference: street drugs, like heroin and catnip, are grown in uncontrolled, often illegal conditions and sold to you by untrustworthy criminals and foreigners. Prescription drugs, on the other hand, are manufactured under highly controlled conditions as dictated by the one-world government cronies at big pharma, as part of their mind-control program for the purpose of rendering our cats weak and docile. Whether grown in a field for greed or in a lab to subjugate the world, both street drugs and prescription medications are evil and should be kept as far from your cat as possible!

What happens when a cat's life has been ruined by catnip?

It is impossible to understand the true horror that awaits kittens on the path of drug addiction through statistics and graphs alone. Sometimes a more *purr*sonal touch is necessary. We would like to share with you this story, which was sent to us from the front lines of the war on drugs:

His name was Professor Fluffyface. He was a bright and promising young kitten who loved getting his chin scratched, climbing trees, and chasing bugs. Then one fateful day his best friend, Snickers Pussyfoot, stopped by for a visit while his owners were out. Snickers was eager to show Fluffyface his newest toy: a fake mouse stuffed with catnip. Unfortunately for the Professor, while his owners had taught him many important lessons about the safe handling of firearms and using the Internet responsibly, they had never thought to warn him against the dangers of catnip or other illegal drugs. All he knew was what he had seen on TV: that using catnip made you a "cool cat." Professor Fluffyface said yes, and within seconds of his first nibble on that mouse, he was addicted and his life began to spiral out of control. Catnip quickly consumed his every waking thought. Gone were the days of perching on branches, feeling the wind ruffle his whiskers. Now his life revolved around another kind of high: being high on drugs. It wasn't long before Fluffyface began stealing from his owners to pay for his catnip habit. First, it was just pulling money out of their wallets in the wee hours of the night, but not long after that he was hocking their TV to pay for his addiction, and soon he tried his paw at cat burglary. It was only a matter of time before he was caught and his owners kicked him out. He was homeless, addicted, and forced to offer his body for sale. Professor Fluffyface would have given anything to have gone back to his old life—nowadays the only chin scratches he got were from strange men in seedy motel rooms—but catnip wasn't done with him yet! One night a "customer" got rough with him and tried to pet Fluffyface's fur the wrong way. The claws came out, and seconds later Professor Flufflyface had committed the worst crime a cat can be convicted of: furst degree purrder! Two souls lost that night, and it all started with one little catnip mouse.

Don't let this sad story be your cat's tail! Talk to them about the dangers of drug use today!

Behold the heartbreaking descent of Professor Fluffyface.

Is it true that some owners give their cats drugs on purpose?

Sadly, yes. While there are a few owners out there who give their cats drugs because of some sadistic sense of humor, most are just ignorant, completely unaware of the damage that catnip addiction inflicts on the lives of millions of cats every day. These people have swallowed the prepawsterous lie that catnip is harmless fun for your kitty, but make no mistake: catnip can be as deadly to your cat as heartworms or FIV!

Can drugs really be that bad if some states are legalizing them?

It is true that a few states filled with wacko liberals have begun to decriminalize marijuana. But just because it's legal doesn't mean it's a good idea. Just as legalizing homosexuality is a slippery slope that will inevitably lead to people wanting to marry children and horses, legalizing marijuana can have only similarly disastrous repercussions. Just look at the liberals' boneheaded laws about abortion, Obamacare, and the ERA: Jesus should be your cat's moral compass, not the government. Don't put your cat's well-being in jeo*purr*dy because of the wackos' bad decisions!

What is the best way to have "the talk" with my cat about drugs?

There should not be just one talk about drugs and the evils of catnip. It is a good idea to have a number of big discussions with your kitty so you can lay out all the evils associated with drugs. But more important are the many follow-up conversations where you should employ a subtler approach. Don't just sit your cat down and tell them that drugs are bad! Instead, look for ways to inject anti-catnip lessons into your normal everyday conversations. For instance, if you're watching the news with your cat and see a story about a horrific plane crash, mention that perhaps a cat high on drugs was piloting the plane, and that the crash was the result. Or if your cat is using the computer and sees a picture of an unhappy-looking kitty in a funny costume, suggest that maybe the cat is a drug addict and has been forced to sell his furry body in order to get enough money for his next score. Dropping these hints every day will go a long way toward making your cat more receptive when it's time for the big talk.

NOW DON'T *PAWSE* FOR ONE SECOND LONGER! GO TALK TO YOUR CAT!

HOW TO TALK TO YOUR CAT ABOUT
PUBERTY

AMERICAN ASSOCIATION OF PATRIOTS

Do I need to talk to my cat about puberty?

Of course! Puberty can be a scary time for any young cat or kitten. Their bodies are beset by changes that they cannot understand. They're getting bigger. They're growing fur in strange new places. Their meows might even be getting deeper. And without your guidance, your poor little kitten will have no idea of what's happening to them! Your wisdom will be essential for helping your cat comprehend and navigate the changes they're experiencing. Talking to your cat about this will be one of the most important discussions you'll have with your cat at this stage of their life, but it's far from the only one! In fact, the months during which your cat goes through puberty will likely entail many of the discussions that cat owners report as being the most difficult and intimidating. It is during these months you will frequently need to talk to your cat about topics that brush upon morality, sexuality, and responsibility. How you handle these discussions will likely determine what sort of cat your kitten grows up to be. Will they be a hardworking cat who loves God, America, and belly rubs? Or will they be a degenerate, lazy alley cat, too high on catnip to bother looking for a job? The stakes for your kitty will never be higher! For this reason, we have written this chapter to answer all your questions regarding the physical changes associated with puberty as well as a wide range of other topics your young kitten will need guidance on if they are to grow into a cat who will make America *purroud*—from video games and masturbation to bullying and homosexuality.

How can I talk to my cat about the changes their body will be experiencing?

Kittens grow up so fast. It seems like just the other day they were opening their eyes for the first time, or finally getting big enough that you were no longer worried about their mother eating them. But before you know it, it's time for "The Talk." Puberty can be a strange and confusing time for kittens. Humans are bewildered by the experience with an entire dozen years to prepare—kittens enter puberty at as young as four months old!

Almost universally, cat owners report that talking to their pets about puberty and sex is awkward and uncomfortable; sometimes owners even put it off in hopes that their kitten will learn what they need to know at school instead. But think for a moment: if American schoolteachers are unable to hang a copy of the Ten Commandments on the wall, or lead your kitten in prayer, how do you expect them to be able to teach your kitten what they really need to know? The fact of the matter is, as unpleasant as having the conversation may be, no one can talk to your cat about puberty the way you can. The good news is that it's easier than you think! Every day we hear from cat owners who are worried about saying the wrong thing. Such fears are almost always ungrounded: you'll be fine as long as you explain to your kitten that the changes they're experiencing are a normal part of growing up that every cat goes through, and that any sexual urges they might be experiencing are sinful and wrong and if they act on them they'll become dirty in a way they can never lick clean. With these two lessons as your foundation, you can't *pawsibly* go wrong!

I have a female kitten. Are there any special challenges my cat will face during her development?

Puberty can be an especially difficult time for female cats. Girl kittens often begin to mature several months before their male counterparts. This difference in physical development can lead to uncomfortable moments around the litter box when they feel as if all eyes are upon their strange new body. Puberty is hard enough for your little *purr*incess without her feeling as if she's the only one it's happening to! It's important to talk to your cat early on and reassure her that even though it might be happening at a different pace, puberty is something that all cats experience, and feeling self-conscious is completely natural. Unfortunately, this awkwardness will be nothing compared to when your female kitten goes into heat for the first time! Going into heat is the cat version of getting a period and is how God punishes girl cats for Eve's sin in the Garden of Eden. Just like human women, cats in heat will behave in erratic or irrational ways as their brain becomes addled with female hormones. Unlike humans, cats in heat will become obsessed with mating. If you have an inside cat, she will be *purr*sistent in her attempts to get out, to say the least! It is essential that when your little kitten goes into heat, you keep her inside so as to protect her purity. She will be confused— and possibly scared—the first time this happens. When it finally does, you just need to give her lots of cuddles and love and let her know that even though it's *fur*ightening, the overwhelming devil-inspired madness within her will be over soon.

What about boy kittens?

While talking to female kittens about puberty is especially challenging, due to their fragile and delicate dispositions, talking to your tomcat is still no easy feat! Don't simply have the conversation while your kitty lounges on the couch or sits on his cat tower. This discussion will help guide your kitten into manhood, and should be treated with importance accordingly. We find that there is no better way to have the talk with your little guy than to take your cat camping. A retreat to the great outdoors will provide the perfect backdrop for teaching your cat about ruggedness, strength, and the importance of hard work and personal responsibility, all necessary lessons for transforming your little kitten into a courageous lion!

What can I do if I suspect my kitten is being bullied?

Being the victim of bullying is one of the most dangerous and isolating things that can happen to a cat or kitten. Often disguised as harmless play when they're very young, bullying becomes much more damaging as cats grow older, and it can soon leave wounds that hurt worse than the swipe of the sharpest claw. Bullying can negatively impact your cat's self-esteem, and bullied cats are known for becoming withdrawn and resentful. This is a dangerous path for your cat, one that can lead to depression, anger, and too often the tragedy of school shootings. Here are some warning signs to watch out for:

★ Does your cat seem especially reluctant to attend school?

★ Are they scratching up the sofa more than usual, or pooping outside their litter box?

★ Has your cat started wearing a black trench coat?

★ Do they affect the "goth" lifestyle? (Note, this can be difficult to determine with black cats.)

If you answered yes to any of these, your cat could be on a path toward tragedy! It is important to make your cat understand how serious bullying is, and what dire consequences there can be if left unchecked. Explain to your cat that only losers get bullied, and that they should try harder to fit in and be popular in order to avoid the ridicule of their peers.

What should I do if I suspect my kitten is masturbating?

Let's face facts: virtually all cats have masturbated at one point or another. Even worse, many young cats and kittens masturbate on a regular basis. And not just boy cats! Research shows that because of modern lax attitudes toward morality, females—both cat and human—have begun to masturbate as well. This can be an incredibly tricky topic, but if you play your cards right, you can teach your cat a bigger lesson about life as well as convincing them not to wantonly lick or rub their genitals. Use the topic of masturbation to let your cat know that God has a greater destiny for them. The goal of sex is procreation—to make more kittens for God to shine his light upon. Therefore, masturbation is a waste of your cat's energy, and incompatible with God's *purr*pose for them. Explain to your kitten that masturbation is a test that God gives each of us to see how smart we are. Some cats excel and redirect their sexual energies toward Jesus and being good, hardworking citizens, whereas others fail and want nothing more in life than to bat at their genitals as if they were a ball of yarn.

ADVICE FROM OUR EX*PURR*TS

Enter a pet store at any mall in the country and you can't help but be scandalized by the outfits kittens wear these days. It seems as if girl cats are wearing clothes that, back in our day, wouldn't even have been considered bathing suits! Your cat may beg for the hottest trendy collars, but we feel that there's nothing more fashionable than good old patriotism! Rather than letting your cat dress like a harlot or an alley cat, get her an outfit that will show everyone how *purr*oud she is to be an American!

What should I do if I discover my kitten has been sexting?

Many cat owners naively believe that there's no way their precious little kitty might be sexting. "She's too young!" an owner might say. "He's too innocent!" "Cats don't know how to use cell phones!" But if you think your cat isn't sharing naked pictures of themselves online right now, you are *kitten* yourself! Studies show that almost half of all cats in American households have sent or received at least one sexually explicit text message or photo within the past year. Some kitties do it because they want to be popular, others because another cat pressures them into it. Regardless of the reason, these are not bad cats. They are young and misguided, and often don't realize sexting can have grave consequences that will follow them for the rest of their nine lives.

If caught, your kitten may try to defend itself by claiming that sexting isn't a big deal because it doesn't involve any physical contact. This may be true, but it ignores the dire emotional, moral, and spiritual consequences that can result from sexting! When cats learn to engage in sexualized activity outside of the confines of marriage, it cheapens the meaning of sex and can permanently cripple your cat's ability to feel love.

Sexting can also have profound legal repercussions. Many kittens who send and receive sexts are underage, and even if they're willing participants, legally they cannot give consent. The bottom line is that distributing these images is kitty porn, and texting a racy picture to a friend could easily get your cat registered as a sex offender! Many cat owners are reluctant to spy on their cat's cell phone, hesitate to demand random inspections of it, or are uncomfortable with taking it away completely. However, these are all measures you can and should enact if you suspect your kitten is sexting. Remember: you are doing this for their own good, and making sure they're safe and responsible is simply being *purr*udent!

It seems like video games are everywhere these days. Should I be worried if my kitten wants to play them?

With their futuristic graphics and addictive game play, video games are more popular than ever among both cats and their owners. Watching your cat play with a controller or paw at a tablet, you might think that video games are all harmless fun. However, it's of the utmost im*purr*tance that you monitor your cat's video-game usage carefully! It is well known that too much gaming can be detrimental to your cat, both physically and psychologically. Video games often distract kitties from healthy, traditional pastimes such as playing Little League or sitting in a box. Chronic video-game use can even lead to lethargic, overweight cats who can barely catch a computer mouse, let alone a real one!

Many kittens don't understand just how little privacy we have anymore. Once they send salacious pictures of themselves to a friend, those pictures could easily be shared with all the other cats they know, end up on an amateur *purr*nography Web site, or even be used for blackmail by unscrupulous foreigners!

What should I do if my cat has become addicted to video games?

While gaming addiction may seem insignificant compared to vices such as catnip or gambling, it can ultimately be just as harmful, especially for kittens! A kitten who spends all day lounging around playing video games will have no opportunities to talk to members of the opposite sex, play sports, or chase mice. They may even neglect to clean themselves, a tragedy, considering that few things are as adorable as a cat licking their paw and then rubbing it all over their fuzzy little face. Before you know it, you've got a two-year-old cat who has the emotional intelligence of a one-year-old kitten. But don't give up hope! You simply need to remind your kitten that video-game excitement pales in comparison to the thrills they'll find in the real world. Take your cat to a sporting event, camping, or even to an amewsement park! Just get them out in the fresh air and remind your kitty how much fun life can be.

ADVICE FROM OUR EX*PURR*TS

With their excellent paw-eye coordination and sharp reflexes, it's no wonder that cats love video games. In small doses certain video games can be fine, sometimes even beneficial for helping cats hone these skills. Remember, *meowderation* is key!

Should I be concerned if I suspect my cat is gay?

Puberty can be a confusing time for a young cat, but there is one area where there can be no confusion: the sin of homosexuality, or, as it is referred to in cats, homewsexuality. Whether your cat is a *Purrotestant*, *Catholic*, or a *Mewslim*, all major religions agree that there is no greater sin than the depravity endemic to the gay lifestyle. Homewsexuality is in direct opposition to the Word of God, and so it stands to reason that gays are the minions of Satan. There is no threat mentioned in this pamphlet more dire or dangerous than the cancer of homewsexuality. If you suspect that your cat has chosen to become gay, your first instinct will likely be anger. Understandable, but know that if you lose your temper, you risk driving your kitty out of your house and straight into the sequin-clad paws of the homewsexual cabal!

Male homewsexuals are known for being weak, effeminate, and easily scared. One surefire way to ensure the heterosexuality of your cat is to make him look so tough that the gays will be scared to talk to him. There is no better way to tell those swishes that your cat is not to be messed with than an intimidating collar, a black biker cap, and maybe even a studded leather codpiece.

Gay Purride parades have become common in cities across the country as a way for queers to flaunt their ungodly behavior, many featuring floats like the one seen here: manifestations of their degenerate minds that are so sick and twisted we dare not print it uncensored! There is perhaps no greater sign of the fall of our great nation than gays no longer having the decency to hide their deviant lifestyle out of fear and shame.

What warning signs of ho*mew*sexuality should I look out for?

★ **Collars:** Be very concerned if you spot your cat wearing a rainbow-colored or purple collar, as both of these have been adopted by gay culture.

★ **Shaving:** While there is nothing wrong with a cat being naturally slight of build, if one day your tiny kitten shows up shaved, this should trigger major alarm bells. Your little kitty might have become what is known as a *twink*—a small, effeminate male cat who will often be in a submissive relationship to a big burly Maine coon.

As detestable as the scourge of homewsexuality is, there are actually other lifestyles that are still more depraved and deviant! Known as "featheries," these twisted, degenerate cats get pleasure from dressing up as and acting like birds. God created cats in the image of his own cat; for these kitties to cavort dressed as birds is nothing less than a subversion of our Lord's will!

★ **Cleaning:** Most cats are fastidious and frequently lick themselves clean, but cleanliness *isn't* next to godliness if your male cat is taking it to extremes. There is something unnatural about a tomcat who isn't at least a little bit messy. If your kitty spends hours every day preening and cleaning instead of getting dirty and having adventures with his friends, you might have a homewsexual cat on your hands!

★ **Violence:** You may have noticed that the majority of the warning signs listed so far apply primarily to boy cats. For whatever reason, lesbian cats are much more effective at hiding their deviance. While a male gay kitten will prance around, swishing his tail in an obviously homewsexual manner, lesbian cats have a far easier time deceiving their owners about the sin that lurks within their heart. However, keep an eye on your cat's attitude toward violence as it can tell you a great deal about their secret sexual desires: it's well known that male gays are often sissies who hate violence and conflict, while butch lesbian kitties are tough and angry. If your cat doesn't conform to rigid gender roles, watch out! It could be a warning sign!

What should I do if my cat has chosen to be a homewsexual?

Just because your cat has chosen a life of queer depravity does not mean there's no hope for them! If your cat tells you they're gay, or even if you merely suspect they are, it's important to let your cat know you love them—no matter what—even if Jesus won't because of their horrible sins. Once your cat feels safe knowing you won't reject them, you can get to work using these time-tested methods to replace the sin and sodomy in your cat's heart with happy little purrs:

★ It might seem simple and old-fashioned, but if it worked for Jesus, it can work for your cat: prayer! Pray with your cat at every meal, at bedtime, and before each of their naps during the day. Fill your cat's heart so full of Jesus's love their fur stands on end. This way there's no room left for thoughts of sin!

★ One of the chief goals of liberals and social justice warriors is the elimination of the concept of gender. These radicals refuse to acknowledge the greatness of the good old days, when men were men and women were women, and also male cats were male cats and female cats were female cats. It seems as if every day there is another story on the news about a store bullied into no longer segregating their boys' collars from the girls', or an article about restaurants being forced to provide gender-neutral litter boxes. Many young cats get so confused by all of this that they might not even understand what the difference between boys and girls is supposed to be, creating an environment ripe for homewsexuality to fester! By helping your cat rigidly conform to gender norms, you can remind them of how God meant for them to be; thus preventing your cat from turning gay. If you have a female cat, try dressing her in stereotypically feminine outfits, like a ballerina's tutu or a princess gown, whereas if you have a boy cat, dress him in masculine outfits, like that of a soldier, a construction worker, a cop, or a cowboy.

★ Above all else, be open and loving with your cat. If you must be upset, don't get angry at your poor little kitty. After all, it's not really your cat you're mad at. Direct your anger toward the sin of gayness eating away at your cat's soul like a cancer. While the homewsexual lifestyle is a choice, it's often a choice kittens make unwittingly. They have likely been suffering these feelings for a long time. Your cat is sick, and you can't nurse them back to health by yelling. It is only through love, prayer, and conversion therapy that your kitty might find redemption.

What happens when my cat is fully grown? Am I still going to need to have these kinds of talks?

For most cats puberty will end by their second birthday. But just because there are two candles on your cat's cake doesn't mean your work is done! Being a cat owner is a joy: there is perhaps no greater feeling in life than your fluffy friend on your lap, purring happily while looking up at you with love and respect in their eyes. But cat ownership carries with it big responsibilities! Many of the issues covered in this chapter don't magically disappear when your cat reaches a certain age. Cats both young and old can struggle with bullying, masturbation, and gay desires. And there will be other things you'll need to discuss with your cat as they age, such as their declining health or the importance of setting aside some cat food from every meal to save for retirement. Your cat's education will never end, but if you do a good job during these formative years, neither will their love for you!

NOW DON'T *PAWSE* FOR ONE SECOND LONGER! GO TALK TO YOUR CAT!

HOW TO TALK TO
YOUR CAT ABOUT
POSTAPOCALYPTIC
SURVIVAL

AMERICAN ASSOCIATION OF PATRIOTS

Do I really need to talk to my cat about preparing for the collapse of civilization?

You may think you don't need to teach your cat about the skills of doomsday preparation. After all, with their enhanced night vision, their superior balance, their natural stealthiness, and their cute little whiskers, what creature could possibly be better engineered to survive a catastrophe? But the unfortunate truth is that years of enjoying the spoils of city life, coupled with a growing dependence on technology have turned the cats of America soft—and not just their furry bellies! Many modern cats have all but forgotten the core techniques for survival that were once common knowledge among their species, leaving them ill-equipped for the hardships they'll face following a global-scale disaster—from a scarcity of food and water to the difficulty of finding good boxes to sit in.

Teaching my cat these skills seems like a waste of time. Are we really in danger of witnessing the collapse of civilization?

Almost undoubtedly yes. History has reached a tipping point. Our great nation has been gravely weakened from eight years under the reign of an Islamo-socialist führer who seeks to poison us with chemtrails. The global financial system teeters on the brink of ruin, pushed to the edge by the greed of the Reptilian overlords of Europe. Meanwhile, the climate machines of the Illuminati, operating out of a massive underground complex beneath the Denver airport, have set our planet on a course toward irrevocable ruin. We at the AAP have sworn ourselves to fight, and we hold out hope that there are enough other true patriots out there that we might still beat back these forces of destruction. But we must also acknowledge that the end of civilization as we know it is quite possibly at hand. We face many hard years struggling against the dark. We humans may not be able to see in that darkness, but we have an ally who can, an ally well adapted to landing on their feet: our cats! If humanity is going to survive these twilight hours, we will need an army of cats at our side—yours included!—who are well *purr*pared to face any disaster.

Does my cat really need to learn this survivalist stuff? Won't I be able to take care of them?

People often think of their cat only as a cuddly companion, but in any postapocalyptic nightmare scenario, resources will be scarce and danger will be constant. If your family is going to survive, then everyone needs to be prepared to contribute. Nobody will get a free pass: not you, not your parents, not your newborn baby, and definitely not your cat. All must be prepared to contribute to their utmost if we are to have any hope of survival.

Further, consider that the world will be a harsh and perilous place. You've thought about the dangers that might befall your cat, but what if something happens to you? Have no illusion: it is very likely that you could be injured or even killed in many of the scenarios we discuss in this book. Where would your untrained kitty be then? I don't care how soft your cat's fur is, or how cute their little nose: when the nukes begin to fly, they'll need to be able to take care of themselves. To fight their own battles, and open their own cans of cat food. You may think you're pampering your cat by sparing them from harsh truths and rigorous training, but not teaching them the fundamentals of survival now will be as good as a death sentence later!

ADVICE FROM OUR EX*PURR*TS

There are those who think it's necessary to shelter our kitties against the evils of the world, but at the American Association of Patriots we do not believe in coddling our cats—only cuddling them! Don't be afraid to expose your cat to the worst the world has to offer, including those foul agents of our enemies—birds. Educate your cat now about how horrible birds are; otherwise, later you risk birds teaching your cat a lesson of their own . . . a lesson in murder!

What is the best way to teach my cat the skills they'll need?

The good news is that teaching your cat the basics of wilderness survival doesn't have to be a chore. While cats can be difficult to train, they are also naturally curious. Contrary to the famous saying, in this case curiosity can actually *save* your cat's life! The key is nurturing this curiosity and making games to help them learn the fundamental techniques they'll need to survive. After all, you can't spell fundamentals without f-u-n! Instead of presenting your cat with a toy mouse to play with, have your cat bat around the iodine tablets he'll use to purify tainted water. Rather than having your kitten chase a laser pointer, teach her how to hot-wire an abandoned car. By using techniques like these, the sky's the limit for the amount of life-saving information you can impart to your kitty. Remember, if you do it right, disaster preparation will be an a*mew*sing experience for both you and your cat!

What skills will my cat need to survive the collapse of civilization?

* **Self-Defense:** There are a few core skills that anyone— human or cat—will need after the fall of society. Foremost among these is self-defense. An angry hiss, puffed-out fur, and sharp claws might be enough to protect your cat when they prowl the neighborhood now, but they'll do little good keeping your kitty safe in a world run amok with rampaging gangs of criminals and radioactive dogs. Cats are likely to face a variety of threats that are larger and stronger than them, from the criminals and dogs to hostile aliens and tidal waves. To ensure that your cat is a potent threat against any enemy they might face, you should at the very least be training them on the proper handling and usage of knives, firearms, and crossbows. Training with a light sidearm is a great place to start, but too often

this is all owners will bother to teach their cats. Frequently overlooked is the importance of instructing your cat about martial arts and paw-to-paw combat. You never know what situations will arise in which your cat may need to defend themselves. Guns are wonderful tools, but if your cat's gun were to jam, or if they were to run out of ammo in a dangerous situation, the result could very well be a cala*mew*ty! Don't simply teach your cat to use a weapon: teach your cat to *be* a weapon! There are a number of martial arts disciplines that are well suited to cats; consider supplementing their combat training with *Catoeira, Meow* Thai kickboxing, or the brutal Israeli fighting technique of *Claws* Maga. Not only can martial arts training save their life, but it will also teach discipline, one of the most important survival skills that any cat can possess!

ADVICE FROM OUR EX*PURR*TS

Cats can be dangerous, in more ways than one. Not only are they ruthless and efficient hunters on their own, but with proper training your cat can be a deadly weapon in their own right. Knives will always have a place in any survival tool kit, but for sheer lethality no weapon can match four paws' worth of razor-sharp claws!

★ **First Aid:** Many cat owners foolishly neglect to train their cat in the basics of first aid. It is a common misconception that because cats are unable to perform CPR or mouth-to-mouth they are useless in a health emergency. While your cat might never be able to perform the Heimlich on you, that doesn't mean that they can't provide other potentially life-saving assistance! When it comes to treating minor cuts as well as certain more serious injuries, a furry feline is practically a medical kit all by themselves. Cat saliva has a natural healing agent, and training your kitty to lick minor cuts and scrapes could help stave off a potentially lethal infection. And virtually all cats are innately skilled at reviving humans from a state of deep unconsciousness simply by standing on the victim's chest and meowing loudly until they're fed; in no time at all the unconscious person will be upright and reaching for the can opener. There is really no excuse for not teaching your cat how to administer first aid, both for their benefit and yours. There may come a day when your survival depends on your cat: do you dare risk a situation where you need your cat to apply a tourniquet and stitch the wound, but they don't know how to do anything besides bat the spool of thread around playfully? Not teaching your cat first aid is un*fur*givably irresponsible!

★ **Driving:** In virtually all doomsday scenarios mobility will be of prime importance, whether your cat needs to outrace a gang of lawless motorcycle bandits, travel hundreds of miles across a nuclear wasteland in search of fresh water, or escape a zombie outbreak in a densely populated urban center. It may seem odd, but one of the most important things you can do for your cat is the simple act of helping them earn their driver's license. A cat who has the ability to operate a variety of vehicles will have a much greater chance of survival than one who is limited to running around on their cute little paws. And remember: don't just teach your cat how to drive an automatic. You never know when your cat might need to commandeer an abandoned car, and you don't want to leave them helpless behind the wheel of a standard transmission vehicle, just for the lack of a few hours pre*purr*ation now!

Just because your cat knows how to drive a car doesn't mean there's nothing left to learn. As the oceans rise and our coastal cities become flooded, the ability to pilot a motorboat, a Jet Ski, or a hovercraft will be a key skill for any cat who hates getting wet!

★ **Homesteading:** Not every part of survival training is about avoiding nuclear fallout or protecting your compound from roving gangs of mutants. In fact, the majority of daily life will be consumed by mundane tasks such as the acquiring, growing, and preserving of food. In many ways our lifestyle will revert to that of America at its most idyllic: the mid-nineteenth-century plantation. In some respects, cats are poorly suited to such agrarian work; they produce little milk and are notoriously difficult to yoke with a plow. However, they compensate for these deficiencies by being one of nature's most gifted hunters. Whether they are pouncing on a mouse or bringing down an eight-point buck with a crossbow, few animals match the apex predatory skill of the American house cat. Your feline friend will likely play a crucial role in keeping your family's larder well stocked with the food they'll need to survive the lean winter months. If you encourage your cat to chase mice, hunt birds, and take them to laser tag or paintball ranges, you'll keep their hunting instincts as sharp as their claws!

Finally, don't limit yourself to these four topics! The more you teach, the more prepared your cat will be! There is no end to the number of potentially lifesaving skills your cat can learn, from operating a ham radio to weaving rope. Even something as ordinary as learning how to swim across a river, stream, or other body of moving water could prove invaluable if your cat were being chased by vampires. Never stop preparing, because after doomsday this wisdom will be your cat's best *purrtection*!

What equipment will my cat need to survive?

One of the most important things you can do for your cat is assemble an EDC kit—or Every Day Carry kit—that your cat will keep with them at all times. You may have a bomb shelter stocked with five years' worth of cat food and the most durable scratching posts money can buy, but this won't do your kitty a lick of good if they're wandering the neighborhood when the bombs fall and don't have the necessary resources to get back home. Well stocked with a versatile array of supplies, a good EDC kit will allow your cat to *purrservere* in any situation you could *pawsibly* imagine! Here are a few tips for assembling an EDC kit for your cat:

★ There are a few extremely useful items that no cat should ever be without: a small bottle of water, a pouch of kitty treats, a compass, a multi-tool, and a small Ka-Bar combat knife are the backbone of any cat's EDC kit.

★ Keep the kit lightweight. Is your cat really going to want to lug around a heavy duffel bag full of gear every time they leave the house? Always opt for the smallest and lightest versions of each piece of equipment for the kit. Bonus points if you can attach them all to a cat-size tactical vest, which will allow your cat to keep the essentials of survival close at paw 24/7.

★ There is no perfect EDC kit. Snakebite antivenom might be an essential item for a country cat in rural Texas but a complete waste to a city cat in Manhattan. Tailor your cat's kit to the items that will be most useful, and don't forget to keep weather in mind! Change up the kit depending on the season, adding a thermal emergency blanket for cold-weather months then swapping it out for a bandanna to keep sweat out of your cat's eyes on a sweltering summer day.

Cats may see in the dark better than all other mammals, but that doesn't mean there isn't still room for improvement. Equip your cat with a pair of specially fitted night-vision goggles and feel confident that nothing that goes bump in the night will be sneaking up on your furry friend.

What different scenarios do I need to prepare my cat for?

It is impossible to know exactly what might cause the collapse of society, and you could spend the rest of your cat's nine lives and then some preparing for every eventuality and still not be ready! The best thing you can do for your cat is to give them the tools they'll need to adapt and survive no matter what scenario they're faced with. Still, some disasters are more likely than others. Here are a few of the likeliest situations, as well as the skills your cat will rely on should these events come to pass:

★ **Foreign Invasion:** Should a foreign power invade the United States, our military—weakened as it is by the forced inclusion of women and homosexuals—will most likely fail in its duty to protect our borders. In this situation, it will be up to cats like yours to band together and form armed mewlitias, just as our Founding Fathers intended. Because of their small size, superb night vision, and natural stealthiness, cats make excellent guerrilla soldiers. While the ability to scavenge for food in both urban and wild settings will be useful, this scenario will see your cat's combat training get the most use.

★ **Massive Ghost Attack:** At the current time, ghost sightings are still relatively rare, isolated incidents. However, it would be foolish and shortsighted not to consider that this situation could—and most likely will—change. There might come a day (or spooky, moonless night) when the ghosts of America take corporeal form en masse, attacking and possessing humans and cats in an effort to retake the land of the living. Preparing supplies in advance will be key, should such a situation unfold. Show your cat where you store your holy water and crucifixes, and demonstrate the best ways to use them against the undead. Make sure your kitty is trained in the use of high-caliber firearms, as many pistols and handguns won't have sufficient stopping power to take down your average ghost. Finally, teach your cat to be extra wary when facing down ghost cats; as mirrors of living cats, they possess nine undeaths, making them especially difficult to defeat!

★ **AI Singularity:** With computers becoming more powerful every passing year, it is only a matter of time before these machines link together to form a super-intelligent AI that views humanity as a disease that infests the planet. In a situation such as this, two seemingly contradictory skills will be essential for your cat's survival. The immediate danger will be from the electronics modern cats surround themselves with. Once our electric can openers and laser pointers rebel against their human overlords, cats will need to retreat into the wild places of the earth—far from urban technological centers—and live off the land. Inevitably, computers will adapt and build cybernetic robots to scour the earth, hunting down the few remaining survivors. In this situation our sole hope is to turn the robots' technology against them. Only through the efforts of an army of human and cat computer hackers might we overcome their cyborg kill squads and retake America. To further educate your cat about the skills they might need in such a scenario, consult our publications "How to Talk to Your Cat About Disabling Quantum Cryptography" and "How to Talk to Your Cat About Recursive Evaluation Functions in Neural Networks."

★ **Nuclear Holocaust:** Based on the best available research, it is predicted that following a widespread thermonuclear war all infrastructure will collapse and society will devolve into gangs of mutants that scour the earth, cannibalizing the husk of civilization in search of fuel, food, and ammunition. This scenario will push your cat's training to its furthest limits. Realistically, they—and we—have only one shot at long-term survival: they themselves must form one of these gangs. Engaging in hand-to-paw combat, driving, living off the land, and avoiding the dangers of radiation are all skills that will see frequent use as your cat cobbles together a veritable army of fellow felines. Through sheer determination and strength of claw, your well-trained cat will not just survive in such an environment, but thrive, eventually becoming powerful enough to rebuild our country from the ashes of the apocalypse. A purer America, led by patriotic cats and humans, devoted to eliminating the perverse excesses of liberalism that corrupt our current union.

It's okay if you don't know every kibble-size morsel of knowledge your cat needs to survive. There are no shortages of books, Web sites, and even expertly *purr*duced DVDs that you can use to supplement your cat's education.

I've heard it's important that my cat not talk to anyone about our plans. Why is that?

Once your cat starts getting excited about prepping for doomsday, they will naturally want to talk to their friends about it. However, all your hard work could quickly be undone if you fail to impart to your kitty the importance of not telling anyone about your supply caches, weapons, or bunkers. Postapocalypse existence is going to be a cat-eat-cat world. A single bullet could spell the difference between life and death, so it is im*purr*ative that nobody—and no cat—knows the details of your plans! It may seem harsh, but it will be for the best if you're upfront with your cat and tell them that if they speak to anyone about your plans, there is a very real chance someone they love will die.

Once I've taught my cat survivalist skills they're safe, right?

*Purr*sitively no! Our research shows that in the event of a sudden catastrophe such as nuclear attack, supervolcano, or Sasquatch uprising, the first few moments after the event will be the most important. Mere seconds can make the difference between life and death if your cat needs to defend your home against sudden assault or escape an urban area before the roads become choked with people. When angry Sasquatches are trying to break down your door, do you really want to be delayed because your cat can't decide which litter box to bring along? All well-prepared cat owners should have a plan of action that will allow them to escape at the drop of a hat.

However, just having the plan is not enough. It is said that the best-laid plans of mice and men often go astray, and this is something that applies just as accurately to a plan involving cats. Not practicing with your cat on a regular basis can be just as bad as not having a plan at all. When the air raid sirens blare, you don't want your kitty to be spooked by loud noises, running off to hide under the bed. Your little friend will need the courage of a lion, the strength of a tiger, and the wits of an ocelot if they are going to be a cool cat in the face of danger; qualities that can be gained only through frequent and regular training.

NOW DON'T *PAWSE* FOR ONE SECOND LONGER! GO TALK TO YOUR CAT!

HOW TO TALK TO YOUR CAT ABOUT
SATANISM

AMERICAN ASSOCIATION OF PATRIOTS

Do I really need to talk to my cat about Satanism?

Satan is the one true enemy. He is the Prince of Lies. The Great Deceiver. The Dark Lord. We have discussed many dangers to your cat in this book: threats to their body—from the tips of their whiskers to the end of their tail—as well as the threats to their soul. Behind all these threats is Satan. Whether you are talking about homewsexuality and abortion or hairballs and fleas, they are all Satan's doing. What good is trigger discipline to a cat whose heart has been tainted by evil? What good is abstaining from premarital sex for a kitten who cavorts with the enemy of our Lord? If there is one thing you must—*must*—speak to your cat about, let it be this!

How do we know that Satan is real?

We need only to look at the moral depravity that has taken hold of the world around us to see proof of the existence of Satan. Global food shortages. Cats peeing on the rug. Landfills overflowing with aborted fetuses. These events could only be his doing. He has turned our kitty day cares into cesspools of atheist degeneracy, heathen dens where God is mocked, staff members are fired for even mentioning Christianity, and cats are expelled for praying. With the exception of country music, virtually every aspect of pop culture exists solely to entrap unwitting cats in his dark design. Satan's fondest desire is for you to think that he is a myth—an abstract concept—but he is not. This is his plan! He wants to trick you into believing that he does not exist, that his followers are nothing more than a joke. Then, when your guard is finally down, he'll get his hooks into your cat and drag your little cuddle kitty straight to hell!

At what age should I talk to my cat about Satanism?

There are no tales—or tails!—sadder than those we hear from cat owners who waited too long to talk to their kitten about

Satan. Some held off because they didn't want to scare their cat. Others thought their kitten was too cute and innocent to be tempted by the Dark Lord and his infernal bag of kitty treats. Be warned: no kitten is too young to be ensnared by Satan's bosom! In fact, the devil gets *purr*verse pleasure in recruiting sweet little kittens for his army of the damned—the more adorable, the better! Satan knows that tiny kittens are the most naïve, the most innocent, and so this is when his minions will try their hardest to taint your cat's sweet fuzzy heart. From the very moment they are born you should be praying with your cat in order to protect them against Satan.

Who are the agents of Satan?

The Prince of Lies would like you to think that his only earthly minions are those who label themselves as Satanists, running around in black robes, committing blood sacrifices, and murdering babies in his name. In fact, Satan has many types of agents who do his bidding. Plainly stated, there are two paths in this world: the path of the Lord and the path of the Devil. If someone is not on the path of the Lord, it stands to reason that they must serve the great deceiver. It is important that your cat be able to recognize these pawns of darkness for what they are. There may be many people in your cat's life who seem to care for your kitty: a Muslim veterinarian, a homosexual pet store cashier, an atheist cat photographer, but be warned! Each of these people has made a choice to turn from our Lord, and if you give them the chance, they will tempt your kitty down the same dark path!

ADVICE FROM OUR EX*PURR*TS

The Shriners try to pass themselves off as a fun-loving and benevolent association, with their pediatric hospitals and funny little cars, but this is a lie! The Shriners are actually a division of the Freemasons, an organization of heathen idolaters obsessed with demon worship, human sacrifice, and world domination. If you let your cat get involved with the Shriners, the only place they'll be driving one of those cars is straight to Hell!

How does Satan lure young cats into his fold?

Satan has many methods to ensnare the mind and soul of your cat, but in modern times the allure of magic has become Satan's greatest recruiting tactic. Satan is a master of deception, and he has used this skill to fool the world into believing that tales of sorcery and wizards are just silly, harmless fantasy. Young kittens grow up daydreaming about casting spells to summon cardboard boxes or to levitate magically down from the top of the tallest tree. These spells may sound innocent now, but it's not long before your cat will be dreaming about powers that would allow them to raise the dead and shoot fireballs out of their paws. Powers that Satan is only too happy to grant them . . . in exchange for their soul! These days, magic is everywhere you turn in pop culture, a situation orchestrated by Satan's minions in Hollywood. A cat today can't even flick their tail without hitting a book, movie, or video game glorifying magic. Here are just a few ways that Satan uses pop culture to entice kittens down the left-paw path with *purr*omises of dark powers:

* **Books:** Millions of cats have read and loved the Furry Purrter books about an orphaned kitten with magical powers. Librarians and teachers have praised the series for finally getting cats interested in reading . . . but at what cost? If young cats want to read about fantastic *me-wracles*, they should be turning to the Bible, not devil-inspired fantasy trash!

* **Dungeons and Dragons:** For over forty years the satanic-industrial complex has been using tabletop gaming as one of their primary methods for recruiting young cats. Games like these encourage cats to act out mock rituals of black, heathen magic. Led by a Satanist recruiting agent known as a "dungeon master," games of Dungeons and Drag-

Many cats initially become interested in Dungeons and Dragons because they enjoy batting at the dice with their cute little paws. But what at first seems like harmless fun can quickly take a deadly turn: it is common practice that if a cat's character dies in the game, the dungeon master will demand that the cat be killed in real life as well!

ons are a way for the Devil to identify cats who are likely candidates for his army; the most promising kitties soon graduate to casting spells in real life. Then it's only a matter of time before the cat becomes corrupted by the infernal powers Satan has bestowed. Read between the lines of any local newspaper and you'll see dozens of stories about people behaving strangely, in ways that can only be explained by cats casting mind-control spells on them.

★ **Video Games:** There is no shorter path to Satan's embrace than through video games that involve practicing magic and casting spells. Demons and witchcraft are common elements in role-playing video games especially. If you find one of these games in your house, destroy it immediately! Such games can have a profoundly damaging impact on the moral and psychological well-being of a young cat. Explain to your kitty that these types of games pose a significant threat, and that such mature themes are not appropriate for cats of any age. Instead, encourage your kitten to try games that celebrate themes that make America great—such as our military or capitalism—by playing Call of Duty or Grand Theft Auto.

★ **Television:** Cats love seeing other cats on TV. Satan knows that there's a shortage of kitties in the media for our cats to identify with, and so when one does appear on television, you know they're there to further Satan's goals. This is why cats are often seen in the company of wizards and witches on TV, from Miss Kitty Fantastico on *Buffy the Vampire Slayer* to Salem on *Sabrina, the Teenage Witch*. There is perhaps no more glaring example of this than Azrael, the pet cat of Gargamel, from the cartoon—and now movie—*The Smurfs*. The character of Azrael is Satan at his most brazen: not only does Azrael aid Gargamel in his evil spells, but Azrael is named for one of Satan's most-trusted demons—a fine role model for America's cats indeed!

What other ways does Satan use the promise of magic to entice cats?

One trendy "religion" that is rapidly gaining in popularity is the cult of Wicca. In actuality, Wicca is merely watered-down Satanism, luring foolish young women with liberal arts degrees into lesbian covens where they worship a goddess and their menses. In many ways these misguided women are almost pathetically sad, but at the same time they are also extremely dangerous. Overwhelmingly, Wiccans are angry, lonely feminist spinsters, and therefore likely to own lots of cats—cats they indoctrinate with their heathen pro*purr*ganda!

I've heard that Satan uses music to turn cats against the Lord. Is this true?

While listening to strange music to annoy your parents is nothing new for cats or humans, the noise being produced today is far more dangerous than anything heard before. Teenage cats can be very impressionable, and it's at this age that they're most likely to fall under the sway of the modern siren songs of Satan: "gangsta" rap, free jazz, and, worst of all, heavy metal. Halfway between kittenhood and adulthood, young cats become confused as they struggle to figure out ways to stake out a new, more mature identity for themselves. They're not yet ready to put away their kitten toys, but yearn to be given adult privileges like being allowed outside. Music has always been one of the most popular ways for young cats to rebel, but be warned: heavy metal *mew*sicians are disciples of the Devil, preying on the uncertainty of young cats to enslave them for an unholy cause.

If you discover your cat listening to heavy metal music, explain to them that while they may think their music is cool, it's actually made by traitors and heathens who hate America and want to brainwash your cat into accepting a life of drugs, violence, and perversion. Once they understand this threat, the two of you can bond by burning your cat's collection of satanic CDs, shirts, posters, and other merchandise that bears the mark of the beast. Afterward, you and your cat can celebrate their freedom by shopping for new music made by true patriots, like Toby Keith, John Philip Sousa, or Ted Nugent.

Black mewtal is a satanic genre of music developed by Norwegian Forest Cats in the early 1990s; popular bands such as *Furzum*, Em*purr*or and *Mew*hem are known for performing in what is called "corpse paint," as well as their brutal, anti-Christian lyrics; many cats from these bands have since been arrested for acts of violence, including church burnings and scratching at the couch after being told, "No! Bad kitty!"

How can I help my cat guard against satanic thoughts?

Whether recruiting a young cat to join a satanic cult or arranging for one of his demons to possess an unwary feline, it is dark, sinful thoughts that Satan uses to gain his toehold into the soul of your cat. Ask yourself: What's the first thing your kitty thinks about when they open their sleepy little eyes in the morning? Eating a yummy can of cat food? Feeling how soft and fluffy their tummy is? Taking a nap while sitting in their favorite box? Then your cat is wallowing in gluttony, pride, and sloth! The first thing your cat should think about upon waking is our Lord, Jesus

Christ. Talk to your cat about how important it is that they spend the first few minutes after waking thinking about Jesus and how He died on the cross to save both humans and cats from sin. Refocusing your cat on Jesus is the first step to keeping them out of Satan's grasp!

How does Satan gain entry into my cat's heart?

There are many doors to your cat's heart that the Devil will exploit. Negative emotions—such as anger, pride, greed, desire, and lust—are his primary entrances. For instance, if your kitty is content with a simple life of lying in a sunbeam after a long day of chasing mice, Satan may fill their head with dreams of solid gold scratching posts and litter boxes overflowing with diamonds, until they become so consumed by want of material possessions that they're too preoccupied to say their prayers. Satan will whisper lies and false promises into your cat's fluffy little ears until they're so turned around they don't know their

It hardly bears mentioning, but satanic cults are evil places, where members frequently engage in rituals that involve drugs, cannibalism, animal sacrifice, and the summoning of demons. If you suspect your cat is involved, you must act immediately to free them from these influences, or your fluffy friend could be next on the altar!

tail from their whiskers! Or take pride: no one can deny that cats are the cutest and cuddliest of all of God's creations. But what happens when your cat stops spending their days thinking about Jesus and America and instead thinks only about how adorable they are? Satan happens, that's what!

What are some of the warning signs that my cat has become involved in the occult?

* Has your cat started keeping odd hours? Perhaps they sleep all day and are awake all night? If so, watch out! Nighttime is the Devil's time!

* Have you noticed a recent change in your cat's eating habits? Many kitties who have become ensnared in the occult will avoid foods they previously enjoyed and instead demand to be fed meat from animals killed with a silver knife on a moonless night.

* Has your cat started acting strangely around the litter box? Rather than covering up their waste after going potty, a satanic cat may spend their time scratching demonic runes and pentagrams into the litter.

* Does your cat seem uninterested or actively reluctant to attend church?

* Has your cat dyed their fur black or adopted other signifiers of a "goth" persona, such as wearing ankhs and/or eyeliner?

* If you touch a Bible to your cat, do they yowl in pain? Does the Bible catch on fire?

* If you record their meows, do they sound sinister or evil when played backward?

★ Does your cat seem unusually angry? Do they nip at your hand when you try to rub their belly, squirm to get out of your arms when you hold them like a baby, or seem resentful when you dress them in adorable outfits?

★ Has your cat developed an unusual interest in weapons, outside of the healthy love of guns allowed to us by the Second Amendment?

If your kitty has displayed any of these signs, be warned: your cat may have joined a satanic cult!

Could my cat become possessed by a demon?

Yes! The Bible relates many occasions when Jesus fought against demons or evil spirits who had taken possession of a person. While the Good Book doesn't explicitly mention any feline possessions, that doesn't mean it can't happen. In fact, we should assume the opposite! After all, what more tempting target could there be for a demon than a furry, innocent little kitten? There

For comparison, here are two kittens, one possessed, one not. Looking at the eyes of the kitten on the left, you can see that he is clearly saturated with malevolent, unholy energy, whereas the eyes of the kitten on the right are suffused with a heavenly glow.

is scant talk on the nightly news about demonic possessions, so most people consider them to be something that happened only in biblical times. And that is exactly what the demons want us to think. That way they can take us, and our cats, by sur*purr*ise!

How can I tell if my cat is possessed?

Here at the AAP we often get letters from concerned citizens who are worried about possible feline possessions. Letter writers report that their kitty has started acting crazy, sometimes to the point where it's as if they don't know their cat at all anymore. We hear stories of kitties who have become angry and aggressive, who pee in inappropriate places, or whose happy purr has been replaced with one containing a sinister, demonic undertone. In our experience, none of these circumstances necessarily suggest the actions of a cat possessed, but that does not mean these cats aren't troubled! If your cat is exhibiting behaviors like the ones described above, more than likely they've become addicted to drugs or are being tormented by a ghost.

Satan has tricked us, using TV and movies, to think that wild, violent behavior is the sign of a possessed cat. To the contrary, demons are often rational (albeit evil) spirits, and are frequently seen in the Bible holding normal conversations with Jesus. After all, if Satan was wily enough to masquerade as an angel of light, then surely some of his minions would use the same tactics! So, if acting crazy isn't a sign of possession, what is? Unfortunately, it can be difficult to say. Satan has different types of demons working for him, each of whom will manifest their presence in different ways.

★ Some demons cause illness, such as cancer, fleas, or crystals in your cat's urethra.

★ Other demons make your cat susceptible to negative emotional states such as anger, anxiety, hate, and lust.

★ Last are the demons who force your cat into sinful behaviors such as engaging in ho*mew*sexual acts, clawing at the drapes, or working on the Sabbath.

At the end of the day, all you can really do is look deep into your cat's eyes and ask yourself if the twinkle within is from the light of Jesus or the fires of Hell. It will take practice! You may need to look into the eyes of every cat you meet, but with time the signs of the in*fur*nal will become clear to you.

You've convinced me: Satan is real and my cat's soul is in danger. What do I do now?

Satan does not rest. He does not waver. He will always be there, waiting for your cat's moment of weakness. He may hide behind the litter box, under the bed, or in your cat's favorite tree. You never know when he will strike and drag your kitty to hell, thus condemning your furry little buddy to an eternity of *purrdi*tion. But there is hope! Helping your cat resist Satan might be the hardest thing you ever do, but it will also be easier than you think—because if you're a responsible Christian cat owner, you're doing it already! Satan may be the lord of darkness, but he has no dominion over the light. All you have to do to defeat him is fill your cat with the radiance of God's love. Teach your cat the lessons of Jesus. Pray with your cat. Go to church with your cat. Be there for your cat when their belief falters and buttress it with your own. Satan may be the one true enemy, but he is no match for a faithful feline!

NOW DON'T *PAWSE* FOR ONE SECOND LONGER! GO TALK TO YOUR CAT!

FURTHER READING

The book you hold in your hands is but a tiny sliver of our total published work. For more information on educating your cat, please consider some of our other "How to Talk to Your Cat About" guides:

9/11
Abortion Holocaust
Being Adopted
Biblical Literalism
Cats
Chemtrails
U.S. Corporate Tax Policy
Disabling Quantum Cryptography
Divorce
Eating Disorders
Fluoride and Mind Control
Gamergate
Georgia O'Keeffe
Global Warming
The Gnostic Gospels
Grand Unified Theory
Hippies
Hosting a Dinner Party
Immigration
ISIS
Jesus
Learning to Drive
Miscegenation
The Moon Landing Hoax
The Moral Majority
The New World Order

Objectivism
Online Dating
P versus NP
Phrenology
Planning for Retirement
Political Correctness
Postmodern Architecture
Project MKUltra
The Rand Corporation
Recursive Evaluation Functions in
    Neural Networks
The Riemann Hypothesis
Santa Claus
Scientology
Secret Minecraft Techniques
Sharia Law
Social Justice Warriors
States Rights
The Teapot Dome Scandal
The Afterlife
The Articles of the Confederacy
The Lost Tribes of Israel
The Tunguska Event
Thimerosal
Third Wave Feminism
The Zionist Menace

PHOTO CREDITS

the cat, lounging by Patrick Fitzgerald; Cat removed and added to couch image; https://flic
.kr/p/afKt. • p. 75: Are You Looking at Me-.jpg by Sheila Sund; Cat added to wrecked car and
beer can images; https://flic.kr/p/fPAdzZ. • p. 78: Kittens_5 by 1970 Lincoln Continental; Cat's
eyes photoshopped onto a cat in a different image; https://www.flickr.com/photos/39311243
@N05/4273391516/. • p. 80: *left:* Tin loafed by R. Crap Mariner; https://flic.kr/p/jKgDnt. *right:*
#CCC is a breadcat by pinguino k; https://flic.kr/p/bmV93r. • p. 83: *top right:* Kitten by Jennifer
C.; https://flic.kr/p/aGC95g. • p. 85: White lions by monkeywing; Cat photoshopped into
image; https://flic.kr/p/7Rou3t. • p. 93: Too Seksy for ma Chair . . . by greeblie; Photo added to
iPhone screen in another photo; https://flic.kr/p/5Teyw1. • p. 95: Folsom Street Fair—2014 by
Piyush Kumar; Hat and mask removed from center figure and added to cat image; https://flic
.kr/p/p3TTNj. • p. 96: Cat on Olympic Mountain by sburke2478; Cat added to Gay Pride-
themed float image; https://flic.kr/p/5N5gQx. Sitting cat by Gorupka; Cat added to Gay Pride-
themed float image; https://flic.kr/p/4zatTJ. Naughty Kitten by Hafiz Issadeen; Cat added to
Gay Pride-themed float image; https://flic.kr/p/8hxz7v. • p. 104: Fat cat by Les Chatfield; Author photoshopped in candy wrappers and trash; https://flic.kr/p/rWRa. • p. 105: Secrets by
frankieleon; https://flic.kr/p/6s5Kh8. • p. 107: Knife Fighting by DVIDSHUB; Cats photoshopped in to replace weapons; https://flic.kr/p/5xqvC9. Boris flies by Andrew; Cat photoshopped into war image; https://flic.kr/p/Badrn. This is a lousy spa by Tomi Tapio K; https://flic
.kr/p/aXUsqT. • p. 109: しゅたり by Yoppy; Cat image added to jet ski photo; https://flic.kr/p/
a4U1N3. Jet skiing on Calero Reservoir by Don DeBold; https://flic.kr/p/8qMs8C. • p. 117: Ex-
plored by eflon; Hand removed and added to Satanist photo; https://flic.kr/p/7kupfy. NAP 2013.
The Devil by Hypnotica Studios Infinite; Man with devil horns removed and added to Satanist
image; https://www.flickr.com/photos/stinkiepinkie_infinity/9372147743/in/datetaken/. • p. 121:
Pirate by Alexandra Zakharova; Cat replaced man in the right yellow car in separate image;
https://flic.kr/p/dz9tPg. • p. 125: Steel Panther in Des Moines by Ryan Moomey; Cats replaced
singers and mic added into image; https://flic.kr/p/tPMc89. Lord Dying 8 by Jeffrey Pollack;
Drumsticks removed and added to separate stage image; https://flic.kr/p/vkzJjY. :D by ni-
coleec; Author drew eyeliner onto cat image and photoshopped into separate stage photo;
https://flic.kr/p/8PmbZ2. Toxic Holocaust 12 by Jeffrey Pollack; Mic stand added to separate
stage image; https://flic.kr/p/ye6hYV. • p. 126: O Altar by Fernando Dutra; Cat with upside-
down cross added to table; https://flic.kr/p/aBov5j. Black cat by Iskra Photo; Author drew
upside-down cross on cat's head and added image to altar photo; https://flic.kr/p/d2ukmh. •
p. 128: *left:* Newborn Kitten by Torrey Wiley; https://flic.kr/p/e91zeG. *right:* Shimmer (brown
tabby cat) and her two brown tabby kittens—6 weeks old by Helena Jacobson; https://flic.kr/p/
p4hE6h. • p. 131: My cat by Paolo Sarteschi; Graduation hat added to cat's head; https://flic
.kr/p/jLFGoV. Graduation Day by Jase Curtis; Graduation hat cut and added to separate cat
image; https://flic.kr/p/aJiawv. • p. 133: IMG_3461 by Digital Magic Photography; Flag cropped
and used as background of AAP seal; https://flic.kr/p/7ycLSV.

Elements from the following images were used under Creative Commons' ShareAlike 2.0 license,
https://creativecommons.org/licenses/by-sa/2.0/:

p. 5: Colt Python1195.JPG by Stephen Z; Gun added to cat image; https://flic.kr/p/c5V87. • p. 9:
Shooting the target by Gabriel Saldana; Author replaced the subject in the foreground with
two new images and drew birds on the targets; https://flic.kr/p/8q8Afr. • p. 10: Remington R12
shotgun by Mitch Barrie; Gun added to cat image; https://flic.kr/p/qVYDka. • p. 15: 00024 by
Tracy Rosen; Gun image was added to photo; https://flic.kr/p/72QbHy. • p. 25: British Robin
by Loco Steve; Bird added to Oval Office image; https://flic.kr/p/bC5ThS. • p. 29, *top left:*
Turban I by Andrew Moore; Turban removed and added to separate cat image; https://flic
.kr/p/fYVpxG. *bottom left:* Treats now. - #Carboncat by Shannon Badiee; Hat image added
to cat's head; https://flic.kr/p/nQHmhZ. • p. 44: Rita by Dick Smit; Headdress, glasses, and
outdoor concert images added in; https://flic.kr/p/4dmU1g. Beauty/Hipster Glasses by Kelly;
Glasses image cut and used with cat image; https://flic.kr/p/bZZa3j. Coachella by Malcolm
Murdoch; Image used as background for cat image; https://flic.kr/p/bXsNV5. • p. 45: Gatos
de La Recoleta by Leonora (Ellie) Enking; Multicolored cat used in Planned Parenthood image;
https://flic.kr/p/6bXYFC. Jingle bell cat by jacinta lluch valero; Cat used in Planned Parenthood
Image; https://flic.kr/p/hMapD3. Feral cats by Salim Virji; White/brown cat in the foreground
used in Planned Parenthood image; https://flic.kr/p/eYeR9. 0101 - Out cat hunting by Ian Bar-
bour; Cat used in Planned Parenthood image; https://flic.kr/p/96uaGY. • p. 50: Demeter on the
couch by Sage Ross; Author added hat image and placed cat in wedding background; https://

flic.kr/p/4pzygJ. Rutherford B. Hayes hat by Erik Maldre; Hat added to cat image; https://flic.kr/p/f5puYV. If, the cat by Nikolas Moya; Author added veil image and placed cat in wedding background; https://flic.kr/p/vbSZHU. Bride & veil by Madeleine Ball; Veil cut and added to cat image; https://flic.kr/p/758XQS. • p. 55: Anca Takumar'd by Kurt Bauschardt; Photo added to computer screen in cat with laptop image; https://flic.kr/p/fdCUdJ. Calico Cat by SpeckledOwl; Photo added to computer screen in cat with laptop image; https://flic.kr/p/fwGe1Z. • p. 58: *center:* I'm cold mama and your computer is warm by Missy Caulk; https://flic.kr/p/qqr6Fe. • p. 63: MySpace by Lisa Risager; Window, ostrich, and cat images added to photo; https://flic.kr/p/6g4Nf5. • p. 65: *bottom center:* selfie by Harry Matthews; https://flic.kr/p/uH5DYk. • p. 75: Suzuki Carry ST-90 1981 by RL GNZLZ; Cat and beer can images added in; https://flic.kr/p/gTPsu9. Litter by Mechanoid Dolly; Cans added to car and cat images; https://flic.kr/p/fd4QLJ. • p. 77: No love like pug love by Rick Harris; Whiskers and ears photoshopped onto image; https://flic.kr/p/9Q8N9q. • p. 78: Conductor Cat by carterse; Closed eyes photoshopped onto cat in image; https://flic.kr/p/54nUui. • p. 83: *bottom left:* insulation cat by grendelkhan; https://flic.kr/p/apXG9. • p. 85: Landry harness 1 by S. J. Pyrotechnic; Green harness removed and cat photoshopped into lion image; https://flic.kr/p/6pAG6e. • p. 91: Thor, Cool Cat Patriot 7-4-2012 by Don Graham; https://flic.kr/p/ctjFa1. • p. 94: Tetris DS by Richard Kelland; https://flic.kr/p/LaMTv. • p. 95: Cat by Xiahong Chen; Hat and mask photoshopped onto cat; https://flic.kr/p/fJ6ud6. • p. 96: Cat by Andrew Skudder; Cat added to Gay Pride-themed float image; https://flic.kr/p/6QJT4T. Fresh vibes by Martin Abegglen; Sex toys added to float image and blurred out with pixilation; https://flic.kr/p/6WAUSr. GLBT History Museum, Opening Night, Castro, San Francisco, CA, 1/13/11 by merri; Sex toys added to float image and blurred out with pixilation; https://www.flickr.com/photos/shockinglytasty/5372381880/in/album-72157625865714994/. • p. 101: Fighting by Robin Corps; Author photoshopped in new background; https://flic.kr/p/6Dpz1y. • p. 114: Girl Fight Tonight 1 by John Morton; Cats added to DVD case in video store; https://flic.kr/p/5MhYei. Kiai! by Tomi Tapio K; https://flic.kr/p/7Kpj8B. • p. 117: Bonfire by Lee Haywood; Fire cropped and added to the right side of the Satanist image; https://flic.kr/p/7psEmp. Bonfire by Lee Haywood; Fire cropped and added to the left side of the Satanist image; https://flic.kr/p/7iWR8Q. Domino the Kitten Explores Her New World by Pete Markham; Cat added into center of Satanist image; https://flic.kr/p/dmK2CR. • p. 121: Cliffy-Yard by Chris Sorge; Cat replaced man in the left in the left yellow car in separate image; https://flic.kr/p/7WySyU. Sitting Cat by Adrian Scottow; Cat replaced man in the center yellow car in separate image; https://flic.kr/p/5SUHFV. Shriners Parade in Newcastle by KASL Radio; Cats replaced men in cars; https://flic.kr/p/7WySyU.

Elements from the following images were used under Creative Commons' Attribution—No Derivatives 2.0 license, https://creativecommons.org/licenses/by-nd/2.0/:

p. 97: Lulu as a chicken. Love it. by Jennifer Carole; This image has not been modified from the original version; https://flic.kr/p/5qxPRy.

Elements from the following images are Public Domain:

p. 9: Tan cat looking out window from behind by D Coetzee; https://www.flickr.com/photos/dcoetzee/5524799412/. • p. 13: Colonel [William Augustine] Washington at the Battle of Cowpens, January 1781; Copy of print by S.H. Gimber; https://research.archives.gov/id/532886. The Wild Cat by Tallis/London Printing Company c1860; http://www.pastpages.co.uk/site-files/Page16-Prints-Nature-Cat.htm. Domestic Cat by Tallis/London Printing Company c1860; http://www.pastpages.co.uk/site-files/Page16-Prints-Nature-Cat.htm. The Expression of the Emotions in Man and Animals by Charles Darwin, engraving by Thomas W. Wood; http://special.lib.gla.ac.uk/exhibns/month/nov2009.html. • p. 25: Oval Office during Carter administration, 173592; The National Archives and Records Administration and Wikimedia Commons; https://commons.m.wikimedia.org/wiki/File:Oval_Office_during_Carter_administration_NARA_173592.tif#mw-jump-to-license; https://catalog.archives.gov/id/173592. • p. 96: Alamogordo Public Library Independence Day parade float.jpg by Allen S; https://commons.wikimedia.org/wiki/File:Alamogordo_Public_Library_Independence_Day_parade_float.jpg • p. 101: Sarajevo Grbavica.JPG by Lt. Stacey Wyzkowski; https://commons.m.wikimedia.org/wiki/File:Sarajevo_Grbavica.JPG.

The American Association of Patriots was founded in 1973 by Douglas Auburn in Slaton, Texas. Douglas formed the organization in response to an illegal raid of his home by the county sheriff, who was attempting to rob him of the thirty-four cats he kept for protection. He recognized the action, ordered by a town council that had become infiltrated by communist sympathizers, was part of a plot to curb the local cat population and make it easier for Vietcong-trained spy birds to monitor his activities. He then created the AAP not only to expose traitors like the council members but also to rally his fellow patriots for the defense of our great country. In the years since, he has worked tirelessly to defend our borders and educate our cats. The current president (or, as we like to call him, *purr*esident) of the American Association of Patriots is his grandson, Zachary Auburn. Carrying on the work of Douglas, together they have published more than three hundred pamphlets to help guide and enlighten our nation's cat owners and have dedicated their lives to ensuring that the cats of America are the smartest, softest, cutest, and most deadly kitties the world has ever seen.

Please visit us at www.americanassociationofpatriots.com for more infurmation about the American Association of Patriots, to purchase AAP merchandise, or learn what you can do to help defend America.